Sunday SULEIMAN

Elite and Conflicts in Nigeria

A Study of the Succession of the Ohinoyiship in Ebiraland, Kogi State of Nigeria

VDM Verlag Dr. Müller

Impressum/Imprint (nur für Deutschland/ only for Germany)
Bibliografische Information der Deutschen Nationalbibliothek: Die Deutsche Nationalbibliothek verzeichnet diese Publikation in der Deutschen Nationalbibliografie; detaillierte bibliografische Daten sind im Internet über http://dnb.d-nb.de abrufbar.

Alle in diesem Buch genannten Marken und Produktnamen unterliegen warenzeichen-, marken- oder patentrechtlichem Schutz bzw. sind Warenzeichen oder eingetragene Warenzeichen der jeweiligen Inhaber. Die Wiedergabe von Marken, Produktnamen, Gebrauchsnamen, Handelsnamen, Warenbezeichnungen u.s.w. in diesem Werk berechtigt auch ohne besondere Kennzeichnung nicht zu der Annahme, dass solche Namen im Sinne der Warenzeichen- und Markenschutzgesetzgebung als frei zu betrachten wären und daher von jedermann benutzt werden dürften.

Coverbild: www.ingimage.com

Verlag: VDM Verlag Dr. Müller Aktiengesellschaft & Co. KG
Dudweiler Landstr. 99, 66123 Saarbrücken, Deutschland
Telefon +49 681 9100-698, Telefax +49 681 9100-988
Email: info@vdm-verlag.de

Herstellung in Deutschland:
Schaltungsdienst Lange o.H.G., Berlin
Books on Demand GmbH, Norderstedt
Reha GmbH, Saarbrücken
Amazon Distribution GmbH, Leipzig
ISBN: 978-3-639-26912-3

Imprint (only for USA, GB)
Bibliographic information published by the Deutsche Nationalbibliothek: The Deutsche Nationalbibliothek lists this publication in the Deutsche Nationalbibliografie; detailed bibliographic data are available in the Internet at http://dnb.d-nb.de.

Any brand names and product names mentioned in this book are subject to trademark, brand or patent protection and are trademarks or registered trademarks of their respective holders. The use of brand names, product names, common names, trade names, product descriptions etc. even without a particular marking in this works is in no way to be construed to mean that such names may be regarded as unrestricted in respect of trademark and brand protection legislation and could thus be used by anyone.

Cover image: www.ingimage.com

Publisher: VDM Verlag Dr. Müller Aktiengesellschaft & Co. KG
Dudweiler Landstr. 99, 66123 Saarbrücken, Germany
Phone +49 681 9100-698, Fax +49 681 9100-988
Email: info@vdm-publishing.com

Printed in the U.S.A.
Printed in the U.K. by (see last page)
ISBN: 978-3-639-26912-3

Copyright © 2010 by the author and VDM Verlag Dr. Müller Aktiengesellschaft & Co. KG and licensors
All rights reserved. Saarbrücken 2010

FOREWORD

Chieftaincy is increasingly seen as a repository of genuine authentic principles of societal self-government, indigenous democracy, continuity, stability, historical legitimacy and cultural identity.

These views came to be widely held in Nigeria, in spite of the fact that chieftaincy, just like all other social and political institution, was very often affected by high levels of conflict and, on several occasion, was itself the principal cause of disruptive conflicts like in Ebiraland, as demonstrated by Suleiman Abogunde Sunday in this publication on 'Elite and Conflicts in Ebiraland: The Politics of succession of the Ohinoyiship'. This timely book has succeeded admirably in bringing to the **fore** the struggle by the modern elite to control traditional institutions.

Chieftaincy as a most deep-rooted and pervasive institution at community and sometimes even national level, has occasionally provided a reliable institutional substitute and a clear and consistent focus for the activities of various important players, be they central government departments and officials, politicians, soldiers, businessmen, ethnic or confessional interests.

The prestige of chieftaincy and its enduring characteristics as a gateway to power and resources have been clearly demonstrated by the widespread of hectic competition among the Ebi**ras** elite. While in essence, the centralized nature of power and leadership is alien to Ebiraland as argued by the author when he says, 'based on historical facts, Ebiras had no central traditional political leadership', but with the modern challenges and emphasis on leadership, it is possible and rational to have a central chief. That is where the problem lies and that is the challenge.

I am greatly honoured that this research carried out under my supervision is being published as a book. Researchers, scholars and students will surely benefit from the findings of this research.

Hudu Ayuba Abdullahi (PhD),
Department of Political Science,
Ahmadu Bello University, Zaria,
Nigeria.

ACKNOWLEDGMENT

My thanks to the following personalities for nurturing my interest in the field of conflict: Professor Paul Izah, Professor Dunmoye, Professor Unobe, Dr. Siddique, Dr. Bako, Dr. Hudu, Mal. Saidu and Dr. Omojuwa. It has been a great experience working with them all.

My special thanks also goes to my family members, particularly my loving wife, Bolanle and my beloved son, Jeremiah for their encouragements and endurance during this research.

Sunday Suleiman

2010

TABLE OF CONTENTS

Foreword	i
Acknowledgment	iii
Table of Contents	iv

CHAPTER ONE

1.1	General Introduction	1
1.2	Statement of the Research problem	2
1.3	Research Propositions	3
1.4	Aims and Objectives	3
1.5	Theoretical Framework	4
1.6	Justification of the study	7
1.7	Research Methodology	7
1.8	Scope and Limitations	8
1.9	Definition of Concepts	8
	Endnotes	11

CHAPTER TWO

2.1	Introduction	12
2.2	Conceptualization of conflict	12
2.3	Theories of conflict	17
2.4	Conflicts and their political dimensions	22
2.5	Causes of conflict	23
2.6	Issues involved in conflict	25

2.6.1 Identity 25

2.6.2 Governance 31

2.6.3 Resources 35

2.7 Conflict resolution 36

2.8 Chieftaincy titles and communal conflicts . 39

Endnotes 45

CHAPTER THREE – BACKGROUND TO THE STUDY

3.1 Introduction 52

3.2 Evolution of Kogi state 52

3.3 The land the people of Kogi state . . . 54

3.4 The history of Ebiraland 57

3.5 Centralized administration of Ebiraland . . 67

3.6 Previous conflicts in Ebiraland . . . 70

3.6.1 Oivo Arimoh Conflict 70

3.6.2 Obangede Riots 71

3.7 Immediate Causes of Abdication of Atta in 1954 71

Endnotes 73

CHAPTER FOUR – POLITICS OF SUCCESSION IN EBIRALAND

4.1 Introduction 75

4.2 Atta as a Traditional Title in Ebiraland . . . 75

4.3	The Political Circumstances for the Replacement Atta with with Ohinoyi	78
4.4	Mode of Succession from Atta to Ohinoyi . .	80
4.5	The Problem of Succession of the Ohinoyi . .	85
4.6	Institutionalization of Ohinoyi and the Transformation of Clan Conflicts	90
Endnotes		97

CHAPTER FIVE – SUMMARY, CONCLUSION AND RECOMMENDATIONS

5.1	Summary	99
5.2	Conclusion	101
5.3	Recommendations	102
Endnotes		105
Selected Bibliography		106
Interviews		113
Appendix A.		115
Appendix B.		117
Appendix C		119
Appendix D		121

CHAPTER ONE

1.1 GENERAL INTRODUCTION

Socio-political agitations are often located in the denial of fundamental rights for security, a distinctive identity, the recognition of that identity by others, and effective and legitimised participation in social, economic and political bargainings. These rights are often expressed and fulfilled through identity groups (ethnic or sub-ethnic). It is the suppression or lack of fulfilment of these rights that often manifest in structural socio-political inequalities, which eventually lead to violent conflicts. Such conflicts or agitations entail an existential component as the aggrieved parties perceive one another as posing a threat to their respective groups, sub-groups, institutions, values and identity.

Nigeria has witnessed several violent conflicts, particularly since the return of the country to civil rule in 1999. There has been a pattern to some of the conflicts. The pattern has been dis-cernible in the Niger-Delta area, Ife/Modakeke and Aguleri/Umuleri. Also in Plateau, Taraba, Nasarawa and Kaduna States. The dimensions have been intra and inter-ethnic. Sometimes it has mixed noxiously with religious undertones. Conflicts among people have lived together for centuries suddenly erupt resulting in mass killings and wanton destruction of property. Matters sometimes become so labyrinthine that the origins of the conflicts themselves are enmeshed in different controversies. People who have lived in area for generations and who are constitutionally Nigerians are over night reminded that they are "settlers".

1.2 STATEMENT OF THE RESEARCH PROBLEM

In the last five years, over fifty communal clashes had occurred in Ebira-Tao District of Kogi State. Often times, these conflicts were between neighbours who had lived together for more than a century. Despite the similarity in language, culture, values and other related identities, Ebiraland is more prone to violence than any other part of Kogi state. For instance, it is estimated that during this period, over 1000 lives and property worth several millions of Naira including the popular Bariki market in Okene, have been destroyed[1]. Virtually all the communities in the Districts have experienced clan related conflicts; there have been clashes between the Ihima and the Adavi, the Adavi and the Okengwe, the Idoji and the Idozumi, and between the Ozuwaya and the Idozumi just to mention a few. The persistence of these conflicts seems to have made many believe that they are beyond solution. Paradoxically, however, the protagonists trace their origin to one ancestor, share almost the same social values and beliefs, and have relations in opposing clans through intermarriages. The main motivation for the research is therefore to attempt to unravel this paradox by finding out the causes of the incessant blood-letting, the specific issues involved, such as the extent to which the politics of succession to Ohinoyiship has impacted on the conflicts, the roles of the elites on one side and the role of the environment on the other. To find out if there is any established procedure or mode of succession, the extent to which the non-existence of any clear mode of ascendancy to the throne could be regarded as the force behind these communal conflicts among the Ebiras.

1.3 RESEARCH PROPOSITIONS

The following propositions are adopted to serve as guide in the course of the research:

i. Resource scarcity and environmental degradation tend to exacerbate conflicts among ethnic groups
ii. The structural inability of certain elites in the various clans in Ebira land to access important traditional titles, most importantly the Ohinoyiship, Ohindaseship and Obobanyiship, account for the incessant conflicts in Ebiraland.
iii. The increasing tendency of the political elite in Ebiraland to appeal to clan sentiments in their struggle for privileged positions is responsible for the intractability of the conflict.
iv. The partisan role played by the state government tends to aggravate the clan and identity conflict in Ebiraland.

1.4 AIMS AND OBJECTIVES

The study has the following as its aims and objectives:

i. To explain in an explicit manner the nature of intra ethnic and clan related conflicts in Ebiraland,
ii. To show how social interactions with political settings have contributed to the intractability of the conflicts.
iii. To examine the inter-connections and multiple linkages of identity in terms of the role they play in the social and political processes including their violent expression.
iv. To examine the roles played by traditional institutions in the political space of Ebiraland.
v. To examine the extent to which elites have used traditional values to advance their interests.

1.5 THEORETICAL FRAMEWORK

Environmental theory is regarded as one the Post Modernist theories of conflicts. A number of major contributions on empirical tracing of the environmental-conflict links emerged in the early 1990s. The proponents of this theory such as Homer-Dixon[2], Mohammed Suliman[3], Aurthur Westing[4] etc, were motivated by a strong emphasis on empirical evidence and a "process-tracing" methodology applied to numerous case studies. The research focussed predominantly on causal links between environmental scarcity, degradation, and acute conflicts in developing societies and societies in transition. They posit that environmental scarcity contributes directly to inter-group conflicts as a number of negative consequences such as impoverishment, population displacement, or state weakening is associated with environmental scarcity. As Homer Dixon says "the social effects of the scarcity create and reinforce instability. Under given circumstances, this leads to collective violent actions"[5]. This assertion is correct in some societies that have experienced massive increase in population without corresponding increase in resources.

The common denominator of all wars and conflicts is that natural resources such as land play an important role. Access to and distribution of natural resources have been the object of contention and violent conflict between social groups and even states during the whole history of humanity. The theory distinguishes four types of scarcity:

> 1. *Physical scarcity, which indicates that a resource is only available in a finite amount;*

2. *Geopolitical scarcity, which is the resources are often distributed unequally on the surface of the earth so that some countries depend on deliveries*
3. *socio-economic scarcity concerns with the unequal distribution of purchasing power and property rights to provide natural resources between or within societies;*
4. *environment scarcity concerning resources that have traditionally been regarded as plentiful and naturally renewable but are becoming scarce because of the failure of human beings to adopt sustainable method of their management*[6.]

The four types of resources scarcity can be interrelated. Unequal geopolitical and socio-economic distributions are often a source of degrading behaviour; and the physical scarcity of renewable resource can be a reason for the depletion of the resource capital stock.

Resource scarcity as well as abundance is first and foremost a property of a relationship between groups and their ecosystem. As such it does not designate a specific ecological status of resources regardless of the degree of bio-physical degradation or depletion one might observe. Furthermore, this property of relationships between groups and ecosystem is always and by definition the product of a social process. The theory equally maintains that similar to ethnicity that can be manipulated as political resource, political entrepreneurs and the ruling class influence the perceptions people have of "their" natural resources. Dominant group do so instrumentally inorder to achieve their political goals, which are often linked to illegitimate resource appropriation in a context of state decay. In this development, social perceptions of natural resources are furthermore conditioned by socially defined property rights and by symbolic meaning shaped by the interactions between the social and the ecological sphere. Consequently, the status of a specific kind of resource constitutes a sufficient or even necessary condition to explain violent conflict if the relationship between human being and nature is not understood. In otherwords, environment has the capacity to modify the behaviour of societies and people by causing conflict when concomitant with a number of political, economic and social factors.

Vilfredo Pareto and Gaetano Mosca are conventionally perceived as the co-founders of political elite theory. Their postulations were in part an attempt to discredit the Marxian theory that elites were a fraction of a class divided society. Mosca argued that elitism is the rule of the few over the many, and it was inevitable in all societies. Elite theories use two basic lines of arguments. First, he argued that certain aspects of human nature make elite inevitable and influential in conflicts. Second, he further postulated that elites are necessary for social organisations to function effectively[7]. For human nature, the theory often emphasises on differences inherent in human abilities as the sourece of elitism: some are strong, more intelligent and more artistic than others.

Pareto in particular argued that there were two types of elites: 'Lion' who rule by force and coercion, and 'foxes' who rule by cunning stealth and persuasion[8]. To appreciate why Pareto could use metaphors such as 'lion', and 'foxes', it must be understood that for Pareto all individuals are said to be born with a 'follower'. The 'masses' for Pareto are destined to be followers because they are inarticulate and apathetic. In short, he perceives the masses as unfit for government but they are most times, use by the elites to achieve their own gaols.

The theories are relevant to the study of conflict in Ebiraland because, the area, despite the limited habitable land has witnessed a massive increase in population over the last few decades. Population growth reinforces environmental and societal stress which in turns enhances violence as resources become scarce; it thus exacerbates conflicts over certain resources considered by the elites to be vital for socio-political existence.

1.6   JUSTIFICATION OF THE STUDY

Generally, very little academic work is available on the nature and dynamics of socio-political relations among the various clans in Ebira-land. There, there is a need to understand clan identities and conflicts as well as the roles they play in the social and political process. Also, the study has policy importance as its outcome will suggest to policy makers ways to manage the problems that are related to leadership in Ebiraland because there exists a major linkage in the relationship among people from the various clans in the area and the perception they have of their leaders. This study will modestly contribute to the academic explanation of clan related conflicts in the country especially the ones that have been considered endemic and at the same time open the possibilities of future research.

1.7   RESEARCH METHODOLOGY

This research use both primary and secondary data. On the primary sources; oral interviews with the major players in both social and political settings of Ebira land were conducted. These included prominent politicians, traditional rulers, custodians of cultural festivals, opinion leaders and the various clan leaders across the land. While the documenta/ library research was utilised to obtain secondary data from books, journals, documents e.t.c.

1.8 SCOPE AND LIMITATIONS

The research covers the politics of suceession in Ebira-Tao area of Kogi state from 1996 to 2004. Only three of the five Districts were examined. The three Districts were choosen because they have similarities with the other two. On the limitations, unfettered opportunity was not given to me in my attempts to interact with, and interview some of the notable clan leaders; this was as a result of high level of suspicion and mutual distrust that exist among the clans.

1.9 DEFINITION OF CONCEPTS

i. **CONFLICT:** It is a situation of interaction involving two or more parties in which actions in pursuit of incompatible obligations or interests result in varying degree of discord.

ii. **CONFLICT RESOLUTION:** It is defined as the formative attempt aimed at reconciling, harmonizing, or managing incompatible interests by fostering a process of institutionalised peaceful interaction. Conflict resolution envisages strategies aimed at resolving or establishing the normal state of affairs and raising the level of peaceful, harmonious, corporative, constructive and productive interaction, even with competition.

iii. **CLAN:** It is a social web that protects via certain identified names and praises. Their formal features are totems and taboos. The totems in many societies, which have clans, are mostly birds, crocodile, fox, lion, leopard etc. There are certain things that clan members are not allowed to do, such as eating certain types of foods and meat. A clan member cannot kill and eat the meat of the animal, which is his or her totem. There are certain groups that they cannot marry from. Strict rules of endogamy and exogamy exist in these societies.

iv. **ETHNIC GROUP:** It is a community of people who have the conviction that they have a common identity and common fate based on issues of origin, kinship ties, traditions, a shared history and possibly a shared language.

v. **IDENTITY CONFLICT**: These conflicts occur when a person or a group feels that his or her sense of self is threatened, or denied legitimacy or respect. One's sense of self is so fundamental and so implies not only to one's esteem but also to show how one interprets the rest of the world, that any threat to identity is likely to produce a strong response. Typically, this response is both aggressive and defensive, and can escalate quickly into an intractable conflict. Identity conflicts can be essentially difficult to resolve. The opponent is often viewed as evil, nonhuman and his views and feelings not worthy of attention. In addition, sitting down with the opponent can be seen as a threat to one's own identity. So even starting efforts at reconciliation can be extremely difficult. Nevertheless, identity conflicts can be underated, or even reconciled if the parties want an outcome and are willing to work for it over a long period of time.

ENDNOTES

[1]. **Ebiconews,** Vol.2 No 21, 2003.

[2]. Homer-Dixon, T,'On the Threshold; Environmental Changes and Acute Conflict' in: *International Security*, Vol.16, and no.34, summer, 1994.

[3] Suliman, M, (ed), ***Ecology, Politics and Violent Conflict*** London: ZED Books, London, 1998.

[4] Westing, Arthur. , ***Global Resource and International Conflicts,*** London: Oxford UniversityPress, 1994.

[5] Homer-Dixon, T., 'Environmental Scarcity and Violence: Evidence from Cases' in: *International Security*, Vol.19, no.11, summer, 1994.

[6]. Ibid.

[7]. Pareto, V., '***The Mind and Society***', In: Livingstone Journal.Vol.12.No.45, 1937.

[8]. Mosca, G., ***The Myth of the Ruling Class***, University of Michigan Press: Lynne Rienner,Colorado, 1948.

CHAPTER TWO
LITERATURE REVIEW
2.1 INTRODUCTION

This chapter attempts an expositary review of literature on conflicts, with particular emphasy on communal conflicts in Nigeria.

2.2 CONCEPTUALISATION OF CONFLICT

According to Smith[1], conflict is regarded as an endemic feature of human history. Estimate has shown that there have been 14, 500 well documented wars during the last 5,600 years of human history. Smith also argues that there have been only 286 years of peace during the last 3,400 years of history. In 1994 alone, there were 31 wars waged in 27 locations[2]. If smaller armed conflicts like the ones in Nigeria are taken into consideration, the figure is much higher. Attempting a more detailed record of the incidence of armed conflicts the PI00M Foundation, a non-partisan Dutch based human rights research centre, listed a total of 160 violent and potentially violent conflicts in 1992. During that year, there were 32 wars; 69 low intensity armed conflicts "in which the violence is more sporadic and less intense", and 59 serious disputes "in which one of the parties has threatened the use or made a show of force[3]. Many of these are frequently characterized as internal or civil wars. And, as the UN Human Development Report of 1994 makes clear, the majority of these armed conflicts occurred in the Southern and Eastern Hemispheres.

Deaths are only a fraction of the human losses. Many more people were injured and material losses further increased the loss of health or life in indirect, delayed ways. Just five wars of the 1980 in Uganda, Mozambique, Angola, Afghanistan and Iraq/Iran uprooted

17 million people, over seven million of them women fleeing to foreign countries[4]. Some countries have virtually disintegrated as functioning societies, other are on the verge of disintegration.

In Nigeria, from 1999 to 2004, not less than 2000 lives and property worth several millions of Naira have been lost to several conflicts, ranging from communal to ethno-religious conflicts.

Conflict is very fluid, mobile and ambiguous, put differently, it can mean different things to different people. For example, it can refer to a debate or contest; a disagreement, argument, dispute or quarrel; a struggle or confrontation, a state of unrest, turmoil or chaos. All of these can be used to characterise situations of different social settings-from inner emotional or psychological process of the individual to relationships with or between different social groups (such as the family, town, state, culture, or even civilisation).

According to Mohiddin[5], a conflict arises when parties disagree about distribution of material or symbolic resources and act on the basis of these perceived incompatibilities .There are several points worth noting about the definition. First, it emphasises that conflict is both perceptual and behavioural. It is the individual or group's perception of incompatibility and the importance attached to this, which is as important as the behaviour, which results. And thus behavioural component of conflict is not necessarily or inevitably expressed through violence. Violence is one form among a range of other possible ways of expressing conflict or engaging in conflict behaviour.

Second, in suggesting that the incompatibilities are subjective while leaving open the extent to which they have any real foundation, the definition of conflict identifies a key mechanism -

change in the way people think and act, by which apparently intractable conflicts can be transformed and resolved.

Third, it assumes that conflict as a generic phenomenon, makes no distinction between the different social level at which conflict may occur. In doing so, this implies that the structure and dynamics of conflicts are similar whether dealing with the interpersonal or interstate. This means that insights drawn from one level of social interaction may be of relevance to another.

Fourth, it emphasises that conflict is an interacting, and a dynamic process rather than a static condition of event. This is important because it implies that a conflict moves through different stages and this has potential implications on how conflict is managed at different point in its life cycle.

Conflict is a phenomenon associated with human community where communication and expression of various and unique interests differentiate one community from the other. In other words, conflicts are inherent in human societies. As long as people live together in groups they are likely to have differences of interests, aspirations, needs, wants and ambitions. And as the resources are limited, there are bound to be differences of views on how best should these resources be utilised; and how or by what means. The pursuit of the goals, invariably entail the control, mobilization and subjugation of other people, as well as in interest or objectives. It also entails the appropriation of resources. In the absence of a mechanism by which such differences might be debated and resolved, conflict could ensue, the process by which such differences of views and interests might be peaceful and amicable or violent and destructive. Much will depend on the social, economic and political environment and legitimacy in which such differences are discussed and resolved.

Nnoli[6] argues that "If two asteroids collide, we do not speak of conflict between them. Similarly, the collision of two stones or killing of an antelope by a lion is not seen in terms of conflict...... a conflict exists only when a person wishes to carry out acts which are mutually inconsistent but not inevitable"[17]. People are of different objectives and goals, each always want to pursue his or her goals. It is the differences that usually spark off conflicts. In the same vain, Harry Mill highlights criteria, which categorically differentiate conflicts from other situations. He says:

> *conflict may only exist where the participants perceive it as such, a clear difference of opinion exists regarding values, interests, aims or relations, and the outcome of the conflict must be considered extremely important by the parties"* what constitutes a reason for the genesis of conflict in one area might be regarded as a normal way of life in other society[8].

For instance, why the issue of chieftaincy title and unequal access to state resources are regarded as the major reasons for conflict, sheer molestation of one's girl friend can result to conflict between communities that have lived together for several years.

Some authors are in agreement that conflict is part of social existence and it is needed for social progress. According to Nnoli what is problematic about conflict is its explosion into violence. To him, this is the consequence of the inability or failure to accommodate and resolve contradiction in society through arrangements and procedures that eliminate their negative effects and maximize their positive effects[9]. For Swingewood, conflict is part and parcel of human community; it is the basis upon which development takes place. Social changes, social movements occur because of the conflict and contradictions within society, between the divisive interests generated through the capitalist division of labour, between the social aspects of production and its private control and between the requirements of profit maximisation and human social needs. He further argued that the petty capitalist division of work, based on the private ownership of property, creates the exploitative relation between the buyers and sellers of labour power, and divides society into a property-less proletariat and a small but powerful ruling class based on industrial and commercial capital. Therefore, conflict, class conflict in particular is a necessary element of capitalist civilization[10]. To him, while conflict is generated by the property system, its specific historical form is fashioned by the strength of dominant class ideology, the organization and tactics of working class leadership.

Whichever angle and perspective we attempt to look at conflict, it is a serious disagreement, and fight arising out of differences of opinions, wishes, needs, values and interest between and among individuals or groups. It is a struggle between and among individuals, or groups over values and claims to scarce resources, status symbols and power bases.

The objective of individuals or groups that engage in conflict is to neutralize, injure or eliminate their rivals so that they can enjoy the scarce resources, the status symbols, and power bases[11]. It is not surprising to read that conflict is conceived as purposeful struggle between collective actors who use social power to defeat or remove opponents in order to gain status, resources and push their values over other social groupings[12].Conflict is prevalent within and between social groups, social institutions and organizations, political parties and states.

Furthermore, it is prevalent in situation where goals, aspirations, interests and needs of the social groups cannot be achieved simultaneously and the value systems of such groups are at variance. Invariably, the social parties purposely employ their power bases to fight for their position with a view to defeating, neutralizing or eliminating one another[13].

2.3 THEORIES OF CONFLICT

Broadly speaking, there are three major theories which are often used by political scientists to explain conflict in any socio-political setting. These are: social class theory (Marxian), pluralist theory and elite theory. Social class analysis was the first attempt to explain conflicts in political life in terms of socio-political variables. Karl Marx, the first theorist of social theory, argues that men enter social relationships independently of their wills and that their beliefs and behaviours are largely determined by the social conditions in which they find themselves. The most important of these conditions are those, which are directly related to economic production, and these relationships tend to determine other aspect of behaviours and beliefs including conflicts[14]. The theory expects tension, conflict, and change as necessary for human progress. Conflict between social classes, in particular, as viewed by the theory is the basic source of social evolution. Marx sees political life as a reflection of the class struggle, where each of the participating parties and leaders are seen as representatives of social classes, and as such their behaviours resulting from their class interests. On a general level, the theory is often criticised for placing too much emphasis on economic factors and not recognising the complex interconnectedness of the world.

Just as social class theory is congruent with socialism, pluralism is the theory of modern liberal democracy. The theory focuses on social structures and identifies the socio-cultural forces that influence the political process which determine the structure of socio-political relations in society. David Truman[15] assumed that group is the basic unit of political life. This means that conflict cannot be explained by reference to feelings, attitudes, or ideas since these resulted from group life. Nor can politics and conflicts be explained by the study of leaders, since these leaders reflect group interest and their behaviour cannot be understood from the perspective of group analysis. Pluralist theory does not place much emphasis on the nature of the governmental control. The theory asserts that government is a differentiated, representative group, which performs governing functions for the society. In terms of this theory, political life of the people is organised around the desire by the various groups to further and protect their interests. And these interests are culturally defined and have much to do with what groups possess as distinct communities and what they can get from people in power is influenced by particularistic considerations[16].

Those who have access to political power most times use their opportunities to guarantee the dominant position of certain groups and exclude others.

The major weakness of the theory is that it views each group, as monolithic with its distinct socio-cultural values, institutional patterns and orientations. There is no ethnic group anywhere in the world which is endowed with these unique features. For even within an ethnic group, there are other characteritics such as clans and lineages which distinguish members from one another.

Elite thoery was advanced in direct response to Marxism. The theory explains that elites were necessary and inevitable and that any revolution, which pretended to abolish elites, would end up by simply replacing one set of elites with another.

The theory posits that certain kinds of abilities constitute a sort of elite. Of course, not all abilities lead to economic wealth or political power. However, those people who have most of the abilities, which a society rewards, become the political elite. One of the major proponents of the theory is Vilfred Pareto, who was an econometrician as well as an elite theorist. He assumed that abilities were distributed on a smooth curve similar to the distribution of income. In his work on elites, he divided societies into two distinct groups; the elite and the masses[17].

Pareto developed an elaborate theory of social behaviour based on the assumption that most "irrational" is deep within the human psyche. These residues are basic principles which underline non logical thought and action. The theory argues that the governing elite are dominated by the instinct for combinations, while the masses are dominated by the persistence of aggregates. This is a stable situation since the masses are not likely to have enough initiative to challenge the rule of the elites.

The high level of socio-political organization of the elites makes them highly necessary and needed for any large organization to function. A complex setting, Pareto argues, requires highly experienced and trained leaders. An organization engaged in conflict with other groups needs to be able to make quick decisions and to command the organisational support in carrying out those decisions.

In a related explanation, Gaetano Mosca[18] in differentiating between political systems argues that many organizations depend largely on two strata, those that rule and those that are prepared to be followers. To him, it is possible for families to be in an elite position for several generations thereby controlling the affairs of things in the society.

Elites are endowed with certain qualities, which enable them to exploit certain situation to their own advantage. It is interesting to note that socio political prejudices and antagonisms are most prevalent and most violently expressed in situations where societal benefits are involved. In this case, elites may really exploit ethnic or sub-ethnic cleavages in cornering scarce desirable socio-political and economic resources.

It is not far from the truth that elites normally use ethnic/clan affiliation to manipulate the masses that are mostly uninformed. In many areas in Nigeria, prominent members of the society acquire narrow definitions of official obligations in the process of doing the bidding for their primordial social groups. In other words, a person's (elite) relevance to his group is often measured by the extent of patronage dispensed to members of such a group.

Structural theories of conflict assume that the organization of society itself creates the causes and conditions for conflict. They do not seek to explain the outbreak of a particular violent incidence; instead, they focus on the several forces and dynamics at play which make a society more or less prone to different levels of conflicts and violence. Such theories have two objectives: First, to explain why and how conflict is likely to be initiated; and second, to explain how a conflict develops and endures for a long period of time. A variation of this is the idea of structural violence developed by Galtung, which extends the definitions of violence from direct physical harm to a situation in which the "actual somatic and mental realization of human beings are below their political realisation"[19]. Galtung argues that violence is built into unequal, unjust and unrepresentative social structure.

Structural theory of the underlying causes of conflict is persuasive because of their common sense basis and their broad applicability. They seem to explain a great deal with a few simple concepts. But this strength is also their weakness. While they can explain the cause of conflict in general, they cannot explain why the particular conflict. The school of thought is determistic – they minimize human agency and the possibility of choice, creativity and alternative to violent conflict. Agency-based explanation, in contrast to structural theories, locates the causes of conflict at the level of individual or collective agency, based on human behaviour.There are many agency-based theories, which differ from each other quite markedly. For example, Roberts[20] argues that aggressive behaviour is innate and biologically programmed in human species. A different type of agency-based theory, psychoanalytic,argues that early differentiation between 'self and other' manifests itself in a deep development of certain attributes which focuss on the process of group formation and differentiation, particularly the role that images, (mis) perceptions, stereotyping, and dehumanisation play in the decision making which leads to violent conflict.

2.4 CONFLICTS AND THEIR POLITICAL DIMENSIONS

Conflicts that have an incidence, directly or indirectly, on the direction and content of public policy are political conflicts. In essence, political conflict is ultimately about access to public goods and services. Such goods and services, we may note, may be as a result of environmental policy on deforestation and forest and location and relocation of local council, resources become a political matter, especially when it is implemented to restrict or deny certain groups access. In this case, any conflict that erupts as a result of such a policy may centre on the distribution of the rights and privileges available in the public domain. The key to understanding political violence and conflicts argues Neiburg "must be found in the dynamics of bargaining relationships rather than in the changing issues of the conflict"[21]. The nature of political conflict therefore resides or is situated in the structure of power and the various attitudes or social behaviours that spell or dictate access to it.

It is against this background that Miall suggested four criteria as useful in describing a conflict situation with its attendant political dimensions. According to him:

- *A conflict can only exist where the participants perceive it as such;*
- *A clear difference of opinion regarding values, interests, aims or relations must lie at the heart of political conflict;*

- *The parties in a conflict may be either states or significant element of the population within the state;*
- *The outcome of conflicts must be considered extremely important by the parties*[22.]

Political conflict, however, does not lie in mere differences of opinions, values etc. It is the desire or resolve to achieve those differences of opinions and interests put into action that denote or describe properly conflict situation.

Descriptively, a political conflict can be seen as a situation of interaction involving two or more parties in pursuit of incompatible objectives, or interests, resulting in varying degrees of discord[23]. Tajfel has argued that conflicts "seem to grow most directly from the struggles for established places in the structure of power"[24]. It is the struggle for access to opportunities, to the existing rights and privileges of society, which define citizenship within the nation state.

2.5   CAUSES OF CONFLICT

Conflicts arise because of a perceived incompatibility over material and symbolic resources. Most writers on the issue of conflict seem to agree that the causes of conflict include, among others, competition for scarce resources; differences in terms of goals, value system, and interest; and structural imbalances and ambiguity in coordinating social structures. It emanates from socio political-inequalities, ethnicity, absence of opportunities for political participation, differences in religious inclinations, fragile governmental structures, inadequate civil structures, differences in political ideologies, and competitions over scarce resources[25].

Indeed, conflict is caused by actual or perceived inequality of control, use, ownership and distribution of scarce resources. It takes place in a heterogeneous society where the dominant group, using its power, enforces its own value system, symbols, culture and language over other powerless groups[26]. Causes of conflict are "relative deprivation where a dominant group attempts to enforce its own symbols, culture and language over others in a heterogeneous society"[27]. Lack of equitable share and control of resources as well as access to social services among and between societal groups give rise to power struggles and contributes to rising levels of mistrust and disagreements, which ultimately lead to conflict.

Ambiguity is another source of conflict. This, according to Anstey[28], normally occurs where there is social change resulting in uncertainty with respect to the boundaries of authority and social and political acceptable behaviour. Ambiguity is common in social settings where old ways of doing things are no longer acceptable to a section of community, and where traditional methods of exercising authority are rejected by a section of society that is unwilling to continue to relate to the group in authority in a subservient way. The consequence of this type of relationship is a prolonged struggle of testing new boundaries in authority relations between the dominants group and the subservient one.

Nicholson says conflicts can be caused by proximate or immediate and underlying causes, of these two; it is the underlying causes that are more fundamental[29]. It creates the conditions which immediately trigger off conflict. Though the two sets of causes as suggested by Nicholson are obviously interconnected, it is the underlying causes that are of greater concern. There are several theoretical explanations of the underlying causes of conflict. These tend to focus on structural conditions or on human agency.

2.6   ISSUES INVOLVED IN CONFLICT

Conflict does not emanate from nowhere, it is created by human beings in their interactions therefore, there are various issues that are involved in conflict. Of these issues, identity remains crucial, others include resources and governance.

2.6.1   IDENTITY

Developing a sense of self is an essential part of every individual becoming a mature person. Each person's self-consciousness is a unique combination of many identifications.Identifications as broad as woman or man, Christian or Muslim, or as national of a particular country or a member of a particular clan and family.

Although self-identity may seem to coincide with a particular group of human being, identity is actually much wider than that. There are also collective-identities that extend to countries and ethnic communities, so, some may feel injured when other persons sharing similar identity with are injured or killed. The assumption of an identity appears closely related to self-interest. Michael Keating argues that situations claim that "individuals define themselves collectively in 'ethnic or other related terms in order to extract resources in systems where rewards are to be had from such self identification; or where necessary to defend themselves from persecution or oppression"[30]. Duchacek argues that "people support and identify with persons and institutions that largely satisfy their fundamental demands for identity, internal order, external security, progress, welfare and culture[31].

These identities are not necessarily conflictual. Osaghae observes that "a safe and secure identity formation is not likely to generate conflict; it is the threatened identity that tends to produce violence. And once violent conflict has begun, the possibility of defeat is a further threat to social identity"[32]. Self-interest in the form of self-preservation may account for the violence. Keating has observed that some minorities or peripheral nationalities are prepared to credit citizens with dual or multiple loyalties and identities and the capacity to act in different arenas. He suggests that "Minority or separatist nationalism, involves the denial of exclusive claims on the part of the state nationalism and the assertion of national rights of self-determination for group within it"[33].

The conflict among multiple identities was the heart of the famous Nyerere versus Nkrumah argument over how to build a United States of Africa. Basically, Nkrumah's opposition to East African Federation was grounded on the view that there is a kind of battle going on within people of different identities. An East African Federation would introduce a new identity, which was an additional barrier to the acquisition of a pan-African identity. Nkrumah argued that "regional Federations are a form of balkanization on a grand scale". He suggested that such federation may even find objection to the notion of African Unity. We must endeavour to eradicate quickly the forces that have kept us apart. The best means of doing so is to begin to create a larger and all-embracing loyalty, which would hold African together as a united people with one government and one destiny"[34]. Don Rothchild has argued similarly: "If nationalism is a force for integration on a continent subdivided by hundreds of traditional allegiances, it is also a disintegrative force with respect to supranational groupings"[35].

Nyerere's view was that "changing identities was not as difficult as Nkrumah contended. He argued that it is said, for one thing, the new local loyalties will be built up which will militate against loyalty to Africa"[36]. Yet it is hard to take this argument seriously. Over the past decades African people have had to expand their traditional loyalties to encompass the nation. It will be much easier for them to feel a loyalty to Africa which does not divide their tribe and which in the sense of their own experience is little more immense than their own nations. Graham Smith has suggested that the success of self-determination movement is related to the nature of multiple identities. He observed that "the ability to mobilize support behind the secessionist cause will depend upon whether a sense of common identity is strong enough to overcome identities that crosscut ethno-regional divisions or whether local identity is so diluted by stratification and segmentation as to undermine a share interest in cultural survival"[37]. Jenny Robinson suggests that "all political identities are constructed and are constantly transformed"[38]. Benjamin expresses a similar view, that "the perception of nations as individual is based on the fallacy that nationhood is something permanent. In reality, nations come and go and national identity may expand, contrast, or disappear. Perhaps, the reason for the sanctity of the indivisible nation is rooted in the hidden knowledge: that all nations are divisible"[39].

Stuart-Hall contends that identities appear to be changing simultaneously in global and local ways. According to him: "On the one hand, the nation and all the identities that go with it appear to have gone upwards, reabsorbed into larger communities that over reach and interconnect national identities. But at the same time there is also movement down below. Peoples and groups and tribes who were previously harnessed together in the entities called the nation-states begin to rediscover identities that they had forgotten. So on the one hand, we have global identities because we have a stake in something global and, on the other hand, we can only know ourselves because we are part of some face-to-face communities"[40].

Identities appear to be composed of aggregates of traits. Human Rights Watch puts it this way:

> *No group can be defined by a single racial, religious or ethic characteristic, just as no human being is ethnically 'pure' and no society exists that does not have its immoralities. In many-situations, ethnic identity has traditionally been fluid, such that overtime the issue of difference has been resolved by one groups blending into another for accommodation"[41]*

.

Identity groups are of central importance to politics as well as conflict. Soren Bollenrug and Christensen argue that identities are mobilized by elites, in the struggles against colonial rule; the legitimacy of political leaders was determined by the size of their identity groups[42].

Chabal notes that:

> "competiting nationalist organizations attempted to demonstrate their legitimacy as the nationalists' spokesmen by claiming to represent the colonial subjects. This was tested by the colonial state through elections. Where there were no elections, the nationalists sought to prove before the UN and other international forums their claims to represent the colonies' population by (peaceful or violent) political mobilization. Political leaders most times seek to create and sustain identity groups which they use to achieve certain purposes"[43].

In competing for members, political leaders create identities, which best serve leader's purposes. Sorenson has attempted description of both the Ethiopian and Eritrean "constructed nationalisms[44]".to him, they differ in their descriptions of the facts and in what they include and exclude. He observes that: "whereas Ethiopian discourse claim that Eritreans approved of federation and voted for its abolition a decade later to join Ethiopia, Eritrean nationalist argue that federation was first imposed against majority opinion and later illegally abrogated so that Ethiopia could exercise direct control"[45]. From this observation, politics becomes a struggle to find the combination of myths and ideas that can create the largest and most loyal identity group.

In the Nigerian context, Jega argues, "identities have been historically significant in the Nigerian political process"[46]. Tracing it from colonial and post colonial era, he argues that colonial administration exigencies warranted "the invention of tradition and the nurturing and exacerbation of an "us versus them" syndrome, Muslim versus Christian; northern versus southerner: Hausa/Fulani versus Yoruba etc. Religious, regional and ethnic differences were given prominence in conceiving and implementing social educational and economic development policies and projects under indirect system"[47]. The structural imbalances created by the administration under colonialism was sustained in the post-colonial era, the focal point of ethnic, religious and regional mobilization and manipulation of identity as Jega argued, has never been vigorously used as it is being done during post structural adjustment programme.

The regime of Babangida pursued the implementation of the S.A.P ardently, with rapid and dramatic if not profound devastating consequences for the Nigerian State. People became further alienated from the state when it became obvious that it cannot guarantee the regular provision of basic necessities of life to her citizen. Hence, religion, ethnicity and other forms of identity became convenient platforms of organized political actions with a view to using it to either get recognition or resources from the state. In similar argument, Bangura and Ndikumana posit that "in multiethnic settings, politicians may exploit ethnic differences and prevent broad social issues that affect the lives of the majority of citizens from entering the political agenda in a structured way as in the case in many countries of Africa"[48].

However, it has been argued that the rise in identity conflict is not a non-western phenomenon. Scholars have argued that major advanced societies of Europe and America have faced similar identity inspired conflicts, though they agreed that in many cases they have not yet resulted in protracted violence as witnessed in Africa[49].

The tendency today to describe many violent conflicts as resulting from identity problem is mis-leading. While it is certainly the case that perceptions of identity may be a central issue in many conflicts, this is also used by politicians or political leaders and elites as a way of mobilizing population towards armed conflicts and/or as a way of strengthening personal power[50]. When commentators use the language of ethnicity, race, religion or clan they may play into the hands of political leaders who wish to liken the conflict to identity.

2.6.2 GOVERNANCE

Governance concerns the way in which society is governed, the distribution of authority and the resources within it, and the legitimacy of are in the eyes of the society. Good governance makes violent conflict less likely: Elliot; posits that:

> *The combination of institutions, law, procedures and norms, which allow people to express their concerns and fight for their interests within a predictable and relatively equitable context, forms the basis of good governance. Efficient administration of public resources is additional element... the entire evidence of good governance ultimately rests upon a legitimate use of power; public authority must be*

> *sanctioned by the consent of the governed[61].*

There is a close link between governance and legitimacy in producing networks of social and political relationships, which are stable and durable. Legitimized relationships are those, which are accepted, valued and retained without coercion and which don't need to be maintained by the threat or use of force. To the extent that governments reflect the values and satisfy the needs of those over whom they exercise authority, they will be legitimised. When this legitimacy doesn't exist, or is thrown into doubt, demand for social change can result in political turmoil and social unrest. Some of the genesis of conflicts can be located within the framework of national constitutionalism and governmental policies.

The linkage between government policies, actions and pronouncements on ethic relations deserves greater scrutiny. For instance, there is little doubt that the genesis of some conflicts can be traced to government policies, and/or government's non-challant attitudes to long simmering ethnic tensions. While conflicts are influenced by a myriad of factors such as demography, history, the economy and competition over resources, governance does exert a great impact on how people relate to each other. Governmental policies may also constitute an arena for conflict. Similarly, politics shapes the distribution of resources and the allocation of values. As such, their impact on the contours and substances of struggle among group can be substantial. Brown and Ganguly have aptly noted that government policies are relevant to how groups relate since such policies 'almost always have significant impacts on the course and trajectory of group relations"[52]. Among other things, public policies affect socio political relations through differential impact on policies on ethnic groups. In addition, perceptions of relative privileges or deprivations are also shaped by governmental policies. Even in circumstance in which particular conflicts cannot be directly traced to public policies, the government may nevertheless be implicated in the conflict since its responses or even non-responses to the conflict affect not only the scope of the conflict, but its trajectory and duration.

Any logical analysis of conflict requires an extensive examination of government policies. Institutional features on the part of the state may instigate or aggravate ethnic conflicts. Similarly, public policies may have direct bearings on conflicts since the state itself constitute a meeting point for struggle. In some cases officially sanctioned ethnic or sub-ethnic policies may create the incentive or at least the rationalization for conflicts just as access to state power and resources along ethnic or regional lines may precipitate conflicts. Ethnic groups in power may use this control of the state apparatus to effect measures that create animosities. For instance, it has been shown in the case of some African states that genocide was used to consolidate power or a means to seek for redress[53]. Even when the states instruments are not used to aggravate or instigate ethnic conflicts, state policies are indispensable to ethnic relations.

Government policies have a great deal of influence on the continuous, scope and magnitude of ethnic relations. During colonization, colonial policies directly and or indirectly sowed the seed of conflicts among various ethnic groups. Berman contends that:

> *The state in colonial Africa, within the broader context of capitalist modernity, was the central institutional force in the organization, production and distribution of social resources. It is also shaped by the accompanying change in the social criteria for access to those resources; and the resulting social differentiation between individual's communities........ . This shaped, in turn, the scope of ethnic and identity politics, its relationship with other social cleavages and the complex, interaction of identities and interests[54].*

Colonialists used several controversial policies such as the policy of divide and rule. Such policies not only ensured that Africans were held down perpetually in domination, it also shaped relations among groups of various kinds. Long after the colonial era, the legacy of such policies have institutionalized and reified economic and political hierarchies. Similarly, ethnic exclusion may be promoted directly by public policies especially in a situation where the state is the provider of resources and employments.

In a case where the integrity of the state has been compromised because it is viewed as a tool of ethnic control and domination, it efficacy in addressing conflicts is greatly curtailed[55]. A good example is the Yelwa/Shendam conflict in Plateau State in which the government of Joshua Dariye was implicated.

2.6.3 RESOURCES

Historically, disputes over access to and control of territory, material, economic and natural resources have been one of the dominant sources of conflicts[56]. One event in the European wars in two previous centuries was as a result of the global competition for such resources. The colonial empire building of the 19th and 20th centuries can be seen as a form of resource competition and difference in national economic interests, with those interests being defined in territorial forms much broader than the borders of the states involved. The legacy of those empires lingers up till date, in the form of neo-colonization or imperialism and what has been characterized as non-territorial empires, and the wide structural inequalities between the 'haves and have nots'. It is the unequal distribution of resources (Land, Income, and Housing, Employment or political rights and representation) that constitutes one of the major sources of conflict.

In extreme cases, states or the other parties may resort to military action or the threat of it to gain or defend access to resources perceived as vital for survival. Various groups, ethnic or subethnic, in the past had gone to wars because of the perceived or real threats to certain resources believe to be given to them by nature. For instance, conflicts in areas like Warri in Nigeria, the Bakassi crisis between Nigeria and Cameroon and the recent reawakening of the quest by Ethiopia, Uganda and Kenya to have substantial use of River Nile are as a result of perceived or real threat to deny them of access to certain resources. Most times these have been expressed as political and economic conflicts.

At the end of the twentieth century, the issue of resources has taken a new dimension with the increased emphasis on environmental concern[57]. Today demands for land, fresh water and other natural resources as well as the growing demands for societal values are as a result of increase in both population and consumption. Environmental degradation is increasing this mismatch between resources need and availability, because natural resources and environmental degradation are distributed unequally across the world, various regimes and countries feel the impact of resource shortage and competition more strongly than others.

2.7   CONFLICT RESOLUTION

Authors of conflict sudies have revealed several approaches used to resolve conflict among and between aggrieved parties[58]. These include arbitration, mediation, reconciliation, bargaining, problem solving, and the use of force. Demers[59], for example, has articulated three strategies of peaceful conflict resolution between and among warring parties in dispute. The parties select a third party who acts as a facilitator or a mediator. The mediator has no power to decide the outcome. The parties determine the nature of the mediation process by mutual agreement.If the mediation process fails; the parties in disputes are free to withdraw from the process, launch legal proceedings at anytime, or turn to one or more arbitrators.

The second strategy of conflict resolution, arbitration, unlike mediation, is a private process between the aggrieved parties in dispute[60]. The arbitration process is more formal than the mediation process. It has an element of extra judicial approach to dispute settlement. The warring parties choose a neutral third party who becomes an arbitrator to solve the dispute. The arbitrator(s) is expected to follow and apply the rule, guidelines, and procedures defined and agreed upon by the parties in dispute. The arbitrator is also expected to be neutral and knowledgeable. The parties on dispute must agree on the place of arbitration, the use of language, application of rules and laws during the arbitration process, composition of the arbitration, and legal representation. The outcomes of the arbitration process are binding to both parties. The third strategy, reconciliation, presupposes the willingness of the conflicting parties to settle and resolve their differences with a view to restoring and harmonizing their relationship. The primary goal of the reconciliation process is to create a new moral order based on consensus around key values, which encourage and promote cooperation among the parties in conflict[61]. The reconciliation process, therefore, attempts to adjust and change the embedded values and attitudes of the conflicting parties and steer them towards a shared common values and identity. It tries to overcome the conflicting parties' fear, anger and vengefulness towards each other. It is fundamentally crucial, however, that the parties in dispute acknowledge that they both have a problem and should be willing to resolve it through peaceful means. The reconciliation process, therefore, merely assists them to jointly analyse the causes of the conflict, acknowledge the injustice it has caused, and agree to build bridges between them through healing process, forgiveness, and moral responsibility[62].

Cross describes three models that are used to resolve conflict between and among groups: distributive bargaining, integrative, and interactive problem solving bargaining[60]. He indicates that distributive bargaining approach to conflict resolution focuses on dividing resources among the conflicting parties base on the agreement of the parties. It is an agreement – oriented approach to dealing with conflicts that are perceived as win or lose or zero-sum game disputes. The objective of distributive bargaining is the maximization of unilateral gains or self interest; and each party tries to obtain the largest possible share of the fixed resources. Thus, gains for one party translate into equal losses for the other. The process involves withholding information, opaque communication making firm commitments to positions and making overt threat. Negotiators see themselves as adversaries who have to reach agreement through series of concessions[64].

The integrative bargaining model of conflict resolutions, first conceived by Follett, [65] is a cooperative, interest-based, agreement-oriented, win/win approach. It is an expanded pie-model in the sense that it works beyond the existing resources, aiming to expand the alternative and increase the available payoffs through the process of joint problem solving. The integrative bargaining process involves both concessions making and searching for mutually profitable alternatives. It enables negotiators to search for better proposals. The integrative approach encourages the generation of, and commitments to, workable, equitable, and durable solutions to the problems faced by the parties. The preferred outcome of this model is joint maximum gains. It is a form of third party consultation, or informal mediation that is generally practiced by scholar-practionners. It is a transformation-oriented, needs-based approach to resolving conflict that originated within the field of international conflict resolution such as in the Middle East, Northern Ireland and Sri Lanka[66]. It emphasizes analytical dialogue, joint problem solving, and transformation of the conflict relationship. It is designed to facilitate a deeper analysis of the problem and the issues driving the conflict, including an exploration of the underlying motivations, needs values and fears of the parties. Cross conceives the integrative problem solving approach as it prepares conflict parties for peaceful negotiations; it provides antagonists with an opportunity to engage in conflict analysis and creative problem solving before they become involved in difficult and binding negotiations[67].

2.8 CHIEFTAINCY TITLES AND COMMUNAL CONFLICTS

Prior to the arrival of colonial rule, two distinct systems of traditional rule existed in Africa; the highly centralized system had consisted of Royal Dynasties which constituted the locus of power in these societies and succession to the seats of power is by patrilineal inheritance[68]. On the contrary, the decentralized systems had no recognizable single apical head as the locus of political power for the ethnic groups. In other words, one could not point to a single individual and say this is the chief of Tiv, Igbo, Ibibio, Ebira e.t.c. Instead, the roles and responsibilities attributable to the office of chiefs in these structured systems devolved into the most senior male member in the clan[69].

In all cases, the mantle of headship of the entire group fell on the several clan heads in-council. This constituted the basis of their being described as acephalous. Since the colonial era, the institution has been linked to the politics of most African countries. Various governments; colonial, civilian or military have in one way or the other tried to influence the role of chiefs in political affairs. There have been significant changes in the powers of chiefs both at the local and national levels on account of frequent intervention in the mode of representation and administration in most countries.Consequently, the overall powers and authorities of chiefs have experienced ebbs and flows depending on the regime preferences and dynamic changes in the chieftaincy institutions[70]. The point that cannot be glossed over is that chieftancy institutions have served not only as the centre piece for mobilizing people for communal development or agitations but also the effective link between the people and the central administration.

The nature of challenges to the chieftaincy institution over the years have varied and ranged from colonially crafted mechanisms to break their authority to the imperceptible marginalization of chief.The imposition of Western cultures through colonial rule equally posed a threat to the sustenance of the institution. Busia, noted the gradual transformation of the political structures of Ashanti and how the power and authority of chiefs were systematically undermined by the creeping forces of modernisation that were expressed, in many instances, by the adoption of Christian values and transient colonial political imperatives[71]. Where a central political system did not exist before the coming of the colonialists, they created one thereby creating room for new forms of cleavages.

Chieftaincy in Africa has a pre-colonial roots, or, as in the case of acephalous or segmentary societies, a largely colonial foundation. Prominent among the approaches in chieftaincy studies have been partial theories raised to metal narratives of expectation of the passing away of traditional societies, institutions and cultures. Modernisation theorists have expected such passing away as natural course of things, intune with their evolutionary and homogenising perspectives. Dependency or Revolutionary theorists on the other hand have been critical of all traditional institutions, chieftaincy in particular, for having been appropriated or created by colonial and post-colonial states for various purposes, including repression and the confection of bifurcation into 'citizens' and 'subject'[72]. Both theories have tended to see in chieftaincy more 'might' than 'right' and consequently have wanted chieftancy institution abolished or ignored, in favour of citizenship base on the individual as an autonomous agent. These theoretical approaches are prescriptively modernist in their insensitivities to the cultural structures of African societies, and the future they envisage for the continent has little room for institutions and traditions assumed to be primitive, repressive and unchanging in character. Chieftaincy, these theories suggest, would always look to the past for inspiration in the services of exploitation and marginalisation by the highhandedness of African states. Within these frameworks, chieftaincy is seldom credited with the ability to liberate or to work in tune with popular expectations.

In the 1950s and 1960s, modernization theorists predicted that chiefs and chieftaincy would soon become out moded, and be replaced by 'modern' bureaucratic offices and institutions[73]. The underdevelopment and dependency theorists did not seem to give chieftaincy much of a chance[74], which they saw as lacking in mobilisational ability for social and political change. This view has not entirely disappeared, as some continue to argue for a common political and legal regime that guarantees equal citizenship for all, and for the abolition of the bifurcation into 'citizens' and 'subject' that the invented customs and appropriation of chieftaincy, colonialism brought about. Today a 'renewed boom' in chieftancy is observed and chiefs are taking up central roles in contemporary politics[75]. This phenomenon is observed every where in Africa particularly in places where modernisation is believed to have had its greatest impact. Chiefs and chiefdoms, instead of being pushed into the position of impoverished relics of a glorious past, have functioned as auxiliaries or administrative extensions of many a post-colonial governments, and as 'role bank' for politicians keen on cashing in on the imagined or real status of chiefs as the true representatives of their "people".

Almost everywhere, chiefs and chiefdoms have become active agents in the quest by 'the big men and women' of politics, business, popular entertainment, bureaucracy and the intellect for traditional cultural symbols as a way of maximizing opportunities at the centre of power[76]. It is in this connection that we can understand the growing interest in the new invest in neo-traditional titles and maintain strong links with their home villages through kin and client patronage networks.

In his study of Barolong chiefdom, John Carnaroff observed that:

> *not only was competition*
> *for power - a ubiquitous*
> *feature of everyday politics*
> *and - neither preceded*
> *by rule nor limited to interregna,*
> *rules could not be assumed to*
> *determine the outcome of indigenous*
> *process, was succession to be*
> *exactly according to prescription*[77].

Similarly, in Northern Ghana, the chieftaincy disputes between Dagumba and Konkombas have followed the same pattern. The reformation of the chieftaincy institution was left in the hands of existing chiefs themselves. Therefore, it was difficult to imagine how incumbent chiefs would make changes that are inimical to their positions, moreso; the decisions to create any new chiefdom were also in the hands of the incumbent chiefs, not governments. This explains why Konkombas are fighting against the suppression of their agitations[78]. Non adherence to the conventional mode of selecting chiefs in most societies in Africa does impact on the succession disputes shortly after the demise of paramount rulers, hence the resultant communal conflicts.

Communal conflicts according to Nye occur at three levels[79]. They involve transnational identities, for example Islam or Christianity. They may turn on national identities, or they may exploit sub-national identities such as particular religious or linguistic group identities and communities. Such groups, he further argues "have become susceptible to the parochial appeals of political, national, and ethnic/clan demagogues who hope to seize power in states (at any level) whose governments have been weakened by the flow of the global economy. States which lack a strong central government are the risk for communal conflicts. Two dynamics according to him give rise to communal conflicts in such economically weakened states. First, established mechanisms for mediating conflicting lose force in delegitimised states. Second; identities are seen as offering alternative grounds of legitimacy.

Violent communal conflicts according to Otite are a regular feature of social life in Nigeria[80]. He further argues that they are a result of different values, systems, aggressive competition for land, political resources, and the competition between some community leaders.

Conclusively, as Wiebe has rightly observed, "in each Nigerian community, there are some individuals, who have the clout to start or stop conflicts, these central figures could be politicians, religious leaders, youth leaders, or traditional rulers. Wherever they are, these individuals are able to pull the strings that make communities either function or dysfunction"[81]. Nigeria, like most African countries, is a hierarchical society and social relations within the hierarchical structures, are often bound in socio-cultural traditions marked by top-bottom patterns of different groups, to mobilize, manipulate and channel their members to conflict based on their personal inclinations and idiosyncrasies. Low level of literacy and poverty, worsen the gullibility of the masses, who are often induced with petty rewards and promises.

ENDNOTES

[1]. Smith, Z.K.,'The Impact of Political Liberalisation and Democratisation on Ethnic Conflicts in Africa ;Emperical test of Common Assumption', **Journal of African Studies**, Vol.38.12, 2000.

[2]. U.N.D.P.,'Deepening Democracy in a Fragmented World', In: **Human Development Reports**, New York, 2000.

[3]. Smith, M.K., **What is Wrong with Conflicts**: Colerine Centre for the Study of Conflicts,University of Ulster, 1995.

[4]. U.N.D.P.,'Deepening Democracy in a Fragmented World', In: **Human Development Reports**, New York , 2000.

[5]. Ahmed, Mohiddin. **Democarcy and the management of conflicts and Development in Africa,** Longman, London. 1998.

[6]. Nnoli. O. (ed). **Etrhni Conflicts in Africa**, CODESRIA Dakar, 1998.

[7] Ibid

[8]. Miall H., **The Peacemakers: Peaceful Settlement of Disputes**, Macmillan: London, 1992.

[9]. Nnoli.O.(ed).**Ethnic Conflicts in Africa**, CODESRIA , Dakar, 1998.

[10]. Swingewood, A., **Marx and Modern Social Theory**. Macmillan, London. 1975.

[11]. Coser, L., **The Funcionof Social Conflicts**, The Free Press; New York, 1956.

[12]. Himes, J.S., **Conflict and ConflictManagement,** University of Georgia Press, Athens 2001.

[13]. Anstey,M.,**Negotiating Conflicts:Insights and Peacemakers**, Juta and Co.Ltd, Cape Town, 1991

[14]. Swingewood, A., *Marx and Modern Social Theory*. Macmillan: London. 1975.

[15]. DavidTruman, *The Governmental Process*, Knopf. 1953.

[16]. Bangura, Yusuf.'*Intellectuals, Economic Reform and Social Change: Constraints and Opportunities in the Formation of A Nigerian Technology*',In: Development And Change, Vol. 25. No. 2, 1994.

[17].Pareto, V., '*The Mind and Society*', In: Livingstone Journal.Vol.12.No.45, 1937.

[18]. Mosca, G., *The Myth of the Ruling Class*, University of Michigan Press: Lynne Rienner, Colorado, 1948.

[19]. Brown, M.E. and Ganguly, S., *Government Policies and Ethnic Relations in Asia and the Pacific*, Cambridge University Press: Cambridge, 1997.

[20]. Robert,L., Connel, *Of Arms and Men, A History of War, Weapons, and Aggression*, Oxford University Press:

[21]. Neurber.B., *National Self-Determination in Post-Colonial Africa*, Lynne Rienner: Boulder, Colorado, 1986.

[22]. Miall H., *The Peacemakers: Peaceful Settlement of Disputes*, Macmilla: London, 1992.

[23]. Thomas Schelling, *The Strategy of Conflict*. Harvard University Press, Cambridge 1960.

[24]. Henri Tajfel, *Human Groups and Social Categories*. Cambridge University Press, Cambridge, 1978.

[25] Ibid

[26]. Miall H., *The Peacemakers: Peaceful Settlement of Disputes*, Macmillan, London, 1992.

[27]. Ibid.
[28]. Ibid.
[29]. Nicholson, M., **Conflict Analysis**, English University Press: London, 1971. New York, 1989.
[30]. Michael,K., **Nations Against the State,The New Politics of Nationalism in Quebec, Scotland and Catalonia**, St. Martin's: New York, 1996.
[31]. Duchack,I., **Comparative Federalism, The Territorial Dimension of Politics,** Holt and Winston: New York, 1970.
[32]. Osaghae, E., **Ethnicity, Class and the Struggle for State Power in Liberia**, CODESRIA, Dakar, 1994.
[33]. Michael, K., **Nations against the State, the New Politics of Nationalism in Quebec, Scotland and Catalonia**, St. Martin's Press, New York, 1996.
[34]. Ibid, **Op.cit**. p.123.
[35]. Donald, R., 'The Limits of Federalism:An Examination of Political Institutional Transfer in Africa', In: **Journal of Modern African Studies**, Vol.4, No.32, 1966.
[36]. Osaghae E.**Op. Cit**
[37]. Graham, Smith.(ed),**Federation ,The Multiethnic Challenge**, Longman. London, 1994.
[38]. Jenny, Robinson.'Federalism and the Transformation of the South African State', in: Graham Smith(ed), **Federation, The Multiethnic Challenge**, Longman: Loondon, 1994.
[39]. Benjamin,N. **Nation Self-determination in Post Colonial Africa**, Lynne Rienner, Boulder, Colorado, 1985.
[40]. Stuart, Hall.'Ethnicity, Identity and Difference', in: Geoff Eley & Grigor Sunny (eds), **Becoming National**,Reader, New York, 2001.

[41]. **Human Rights Watch**,'Playing the Communal Violence and Human Rights',New York, 1995.

[42]. Soren, R. B. & Christian, D. C. (eds). **Nationalism in Eastern Europe: Causes and Consequences in National Revivals and Conflicts in Late Twentieth Century Eastern Europe,** St.Martins Press, New York, 1995.

[43]. Patrick, C. **Power in Africa, an Essay in Political Interpretations.** St. Martin's Press: New York, 1992

[44] Ibid.

[45]. Soren, & Christian, op.cit......

[46].Jega, A. (ed) .Identity Transformation and Identity Politics Under **Structural Adjustment in Nigeria.** Nordiska: Uppsala,1996.

[47] Ibid

[48]. Ndikumana, L. 'Institutional Failure and Ethnic Conflict in Burundi', in: **African Studies Review,** Vol. 41, No.21,1998.

[49]. Toure, Kazah-Toure.**Ethno-Religious Conflicts in Kaduna State**, Human Rights Monitor, Kaduna, 2003.

[50]. Agbase, P. 'Managing Ethnic Relations in Heterogeneous Society: The Case of Nigeria' In: **Ethnicity and Governance in the Third World**, by John Mbaku et al.(eds), Ashgate: Athony Rowe, U.S.A. 2001.

[51].Elliot, R.S., & John Hickies.**Ulster: A Case Study in Conflict Theory**, Longman, London, 1971.

[52].Brown, M.E. and Ganguly, S., **Government Policies and Ethnic Relations in Asia and the Pacific**, Cambridge University Press: Cambridge, 1997.

[53]. Lemarchand, R., 'Genocide in the Great Lakes: which Genocide? Who's Genocide?' **African Studies Review** Vol. 41. No 1, 1998.

[54]. Berman, B., 'Ethnicity, Patronage and the African Elites: The Politics of Uncivil Nationalism'in: **African Affairs**, Vol. 97 No. 388,1998.

[55]. Ndikumana, L. 'Institutional Failure and Ethnic Conflict in Burundi', in: **African Studies Review**, Vol. 41, No.21,1998.

[56]. Rochschild, D., 'Federalism: The Limits of an Examination of Political Institutional Transfer in Africa', **The Journal of Modern Africa Studies**, Vol. 41 No. 3. 1994.

[57]. Ekeh, P., 'Citizenship and Political Conflicts: A sociological Interpretation of the Nigerian Crisis', In Okpaku, J. (ed), **Nigeria: Dilemmas of Nationhood**, Third Press: New York., 1972.

[58]. Rubbles, T.L. & Thomas, K.W., **Supports For Two-Dimensional Model of conflicts, Organisational Behaviour and Human Performance**, Ifra, London, 1976.

[59]. Deners, J. 'Settling International Disputes' In: **Management**. Vol. 53. No. 24. 2002.

[60]. Ibid.

[61]. Van der Merw, H., **The Truth and Reconciliation Commission and Community Relations: An Analysis of Competing Strategies and Conceptualization**, Manchester University Press, Manchester, 2003.

[62]. Ibid.

[63]. Cross, S., 'Group Expectations and Attitudes: Three Models of Conflicts Resolution: Effects on Intergroup Relations' In: **Journal of Social Issues** Vol. 3, 1999.

[64]. Bartos, O. J., 'Modelling Distributive and Integrative Negotiation, **The Annals**. Vol. 52, No.23, 1995.

[65]. Follet, M. P., **Dynamics Administration: The Collected Papers of Mary Parper Follet**. Harper: New York, 1942.

[66]. Burton, J. W., **Conflict and Commucation. The use of Controlled in International Relations**, The Free Press:New York,1969.

[67]. Cross, S., 'Group Expectations and Attitudes: Three Models of Conflicts Resolution: Effects on Intergroup Relations' In: **Journal of Social Issues** Vol. 3, 1999.

[68]. Staniland, M., **The Lions of Dagbon: Political Change in Northern Ghana,** Cambridge University Press: London, 1975.

[69].Otite, O Onigwu(ed), **Community Conflicts in Nigeria, Management, Resolution and Transformation**, African Books Collective, Oxford, 1999.

[70]. Boafo-Arthur, Kwame.'Chieftaincy and Politics in Ghana Since 1982' In: **West Africa Review:** No.31, 2000.

[71]. Busia, K.A .**The Position of the Chief in the Modern Political System of Ashanti**, Oxford University Press, London, 1951.

[72]. Mamdani, M., **Citizen and Subject: Comtemporary Africa And the Lagacy of Late Colonialism,** David Philip: Cape Town, 1996.

[73]. Warnier, J.,'The King as a Container in the Cameroon Grassfields', in:**Paideuma**, Vol.32,No.39, 1996.

[74]. Herneit-Sievers, A.,'Igbo Traditional Rulers: Chieftaincy and the State in Southern Nigeria', In:**African Spectrum**, Vol.33, No.12, 1998.

[75]. Linchwe ii (Chief),'The Role a chief can Play in Botswana's Democracy', in : Holm,J., & Molutsi, P.,(eds), **Democracy in Botswana**, Macmillan, Botswana, 1989.

[76]. Eyoh,D.,'Through The Prism of a Local Tragedy:Political Liberalization, Regionalism and Elite Struggle for Power in Cameroon', in: **Africa**.Vol.67, 1998.

[77]. Cmaroff, J., 'Rules and Rulers: Political Process in Tswana Chiefdom', In: **Man** (N.S.), Vol.13, 1978.

[78]. Boafo-Arthur, Kwame.'Chieftaincy and Politics in Ghana Since 1982' In: **West Africa Review**: No.31.2000.

[79]. Joseph, Nye, `International Conflicts after the Cold War', in: **Aspen Institute Journal**, Colorado, Vol.31.No.9, 1995.

[80]. Otite, O. Onigwu., **Ethnic Pluralism and Ethnicity in Nigeria**, Shaneson: Ibadan, 1990.

[81]. Wiebe, B. 'To Build a Nation Where peace and Justice shall Reign', **Conflict Resolution Initiatives in Nigeria**. Unpublished Reports by USAID/OTI. 2000.

CHAPTER THREE
BACKGROUND TO THE STUDY
3.1 INTRODUCTION

This chapter attempts to discuss the political evolution of the state in Federal Republic of Nigeria.It also discusses the geopolitics and ethnography of Ebira.

3.2 EVOLUTION OF KOGI STATE

Kogi state like most states of the federation has a colonial history that dates back to 18th century.During colonialism the territory was divided into Provinces and Divisions designed to facilitate the Imperialist interests. The provinces were administrative units with Residents and District Officers in that order as political and administrative heads under the authority and direction of the Regional Government. Kabba province was then one of such provinces, with headquarters at Lokoja. Kabba province as it was then known comprised ethnic groups such as Igala, Okun, Ebira, Ogori-Magongo, Ebira-koto, Oworo etc,with Divisions which were then headed by Divisional Officers and District Officers (D.O) It must be noted that, Igala Division was then placed under Onitsha Province[1]. As a result of structural organisation and re-organisation that subsequently followed in 1954, Igala Division was carved out of Onitsha province and merged with Kabba province in the Northern Region.

Along with their foundation brothers and sisters of the defunct Northern Region, Kabba province was merged with Ilorin province to form the old Kwara state in the new state creation exercise carried out by Gen. Yakubu Gowon in May, 1967. But no sooner had the Igala and Okuns found themselves in Kwara state, than they started to agitate to leave the state. While some of the Igala agitated to join their Tiv and Idoma brothers and sisters in Benue state, some of the Okuns demanded to be merged with their Yoruba kith and kin in the present day South-West geographical zone of Nigeria. The other ethnic groups, principally the Ebira, the Ebira-kotos and the Bassa Nges, consistently stood their ground to remain as one under their former Kabba province brotherhood even during the colonial period[2]. In 1976 the Igala voluntarily opted out of the then Kwara state to join Benue state, however this much sought opportunity that finally came their way did not last long before allegations and counter allegations of marginalization broke out between the Tiv who are the major ethnic group in Benue state and the minority Igala.This continued until the creation of Kogi state in 1991.

3.3 THE LAND AND THE PEOPLE OF KOGI STATE

Kogi state was created in 1991 by the military regime of President Ibrahim Babangida. The state has many boundaries and contiguous neigbours. The State enjoys the centrality of location, almost in the heartland of the country. It has a common border with the Federal Capital Territory (F.C.T) Niger and Plateau States in its northern side while in the eastern flank, it shares boundaries with Anambra and Benue states. On the western side, it is bordered by Ondo, Kwara, Edo and Anambra. The state capital, Lokoja is a confluence town located where river Niger and river Benue meet on the slope of mount Patti. This is on the latitude 6^0 44' East and longitude 7^0 44' North.

The total land area of Kogi State is 28, 313, 5359 kms it is the 15th largest state in Nigeria with a projected population of about 2, 089, 11, (1991 census). Kogi state like other states of the federation has two distinct seasons in a year. They are the wet and dry seasons. The wet season spans between middle of March and October. The annual rainfalls stand between 106mm and 1524 mm, while the mean daily temperature ranges between 24^0C and 27^0C, during the months of October and March, the state experience the dry season. During this season, the air is generally dry with temperature rising up to 38^0C during the day.

The state is rich in solid mineral most of which are found in commercial quantities. Kogi state has one of the highest concentrations of strategic solid mineral deposits in Nigeria. These include iron ore, coal marble, feldspar, limestone, quartz, gold, delomite, columbite, granite etc. However of all these minerals only marble, iron-ore and feldspar are being exploited on a very low scale. The magnificent Ajuokuta steel complex is still undergoing construction work.

Agriculture forms the bulk of the main occupation of Kogi state people, about 80 percent of the local population engage in agriculture. In the state, there is a wide stretch of arable land for farming, and grazing ground for livestock and large bodies of water for fishing. Food and cash crops commonly grown in commercial quantities include yam, cassava, rice, maize, guinea-corn, cocoa, coffee, cashew, and palm trees. The potential for fishing production is equally very high with over 2,000 fishing ponds and 210 major fishing villages sustained by the river Niger and river Benue which form a confluence in Lokoja the state capital. These agricultural potentials are very good sources of raw materials for agro-allied industrial such as flour mills, fruits juice processing, vegetable oil and soap production etc.

Kogi state is culturally heterogenous with many ethnic groups. The major ethnic groups are Igala predominantly found in the Eastern part of the state, Ebira occupying the central senatorial district and Okun (Yoruba) people located in the Western part of the state. Similar to what is obtainable in the larger Nigerian state where the three major ethnic groups dominate the politics of the country, in Kogi state the named three major ethnic groups consistently struggle for political power at the expense of other small ethnic groups such as Oworo, Ebira Koto in Western part of the state Bassa Nge in the East and Ogori-Magongo in the Central Senatorial District.

Below are the local government councils in the state. They are classified according to their Senatoria Districts

KOGI EAST SENATORIAL DISTRICT

LGA	Headquarters
Ankpa	Ankpa
Bassa	Oguma
Dekina	Dekina
Ibaji	Onyedega
Idah	Idah
Igala mela/Odolu	Ajaka
Ofu	Ugwolawo
Olamaboro	Okpo
Omala	Abejukolo

Source: Compiled by the Author.

KOGI CENTRAL SENATORIAL DISTRICT

LGA	Headquarters
Adavi	Ogaminana
Ajaokuta	Adogo
Ogori- Magongo	Akapha
Okehi	Obangede
Okene	Okene

KOGI WEST SENATORIAL DISTRICT

LGA	Headquarters
Ijumu	Iyara
Kabba Bunu	Kabba
Kogi	Koton-karfi
Lokoja	Lokoja
Mopa-Muro	Mopa
Yagba east	Isanlu
Yagba west	Odo Ere

Source: Compiled by the Author.

3.4 THE HISTORY OF EBIRALAND

The dominant ethnic group inhabiting the area formerly known as Igbira Division is Ebira. The people speak the Ebira language, distinct, but not unrelated to other languages in Nigeria. The population of the Division was 325, 273 in 1963(1963 census) and 722, 032 in 1991 (1991 Census). The people are predominantly Moslems, few Christian faithfuls and some Traditional religion believers.Traditional values and festivals such as Echane, Ekuehi e.t.c are widely observed across the land. Ebiras are also found in the Nassarawa State, in Agatu District of Benue State, in Kotonkarfe Local government of Kogi State and in Akoko Edo in Edo State.

The whole area is characterized by hills, a continuation of the Kukuruku highlands. Most of the rocks are so eroded that they now form a lot of landscapes. The geographical environment of the Ebiras (West of the Niger) known as "Ebira Ehi" (also called the

Inland Igbiras by the British) almost secluded them from the surrounding ethnic groups before the coming of the British. The rugged and inaccessible landscape helped the Ebiras to overcome external aggressors.

There is generally adequate rainfall for abundant plant growth. Most of the rainfalls are between the months of April and November, with annual rainfall of between 125mm and 150mm. Ebiras are mostly farmers and the women mainly engage in cloth weaving. As a result of the upsurge in population growth, the small fertile land in Ebiraland has become inadequate, many able-bodied farmers have migrated to neighbouring states of Edo, Ondo and Ekiti.

The Ebiras had in the past lived together in clans and sub-clans. One could easily guess the clan area (s) or settlement(s) from the type of salutations and taboos prevalent in any particular locality. For instance, in Nkako-Okene, the greeting would be "*Tao-Oziogu*" while in *Ukowa* still within Okene, it would be "*Tao Oziotu*". Some of the totemic valves and symbols the clans indentified with include; eagle, lion, crodile, leopard e.t.c. The reason for this type of social settlement in clans, subclans and strict adherence to these values and symbols was to promote social and political bonds among the members and also to motivate a sense of security. Even in Okene town where urbanization has taken place, this social set up has not changed considerably. The local administrative patterns tend to follow this social arrangement. Infact, the present Districts of Adavi, Okengwe, Eika, Okehi and Ihima were modelled in line with clan areas without central political authority.

There are very few published works on the history of Ebira most of them are based on oral traditions given by elders and traditional title holders. They examine the nature of the historical relationships that existed between some ethnic groups such as Yoruba, Igala and Jukun. Also Colonial Anthropologists gave their own accounts on the origin of Ebira though with distortion and inaccuracy. The origin of Ebira, which is related to the Yoruba, is narrated thus:

> *Two brothers who founded Kabba and Igbira were also Ifes. They left Ile-ife and on reaching a mountain side, the elder brother told his younger brother that he would climb up a certain granary, meaning 'Oke-Aba', later contracted to Kabba' as we know it today. The younger brother said that he would settle at a place near Ira tree ('Ibi-Ira') contracted to 'Igbirra*[3].

This account has not given the exact date and why they decided to leave Ife. Moreso if the ancestors of Ebiras were of Ile-Ife origin like those of Kabba who speak Yoruba dialect, why is the Ebira dialect not Yoruba-like? The political organization, general outlook and behaviour of the two peoples are different as such the theory is hard to sustain.

Some elders of Ebira and colonial officcials hold the views that the Ebiras and Igalas were brothers. This opinion is based on the fact that the Ebira at one time in the course of their migration sojourn stayed with some group of people in a place near Idah, these people later became Igala ethnic group. It was averred that "The Igbirras, of Kabba Province, are akin to the Igalas, and have remained pagans though have a chief who got converted to Islam"[4]. The Igalas were an admixture of Okpoto and Yorubas who had already settled permanently before the Jukun emigrants arrived at Idah to establish the Igala chiefdom[5]. The linguistic connection between the Yorubas and Igalas confirms this statement. Despite the fact that the Ebira and Igalas lived close to each other, their traditions, cultures and values are different. They were only patners (associates) in the establishment of Igala Kingdom.Other people believe that Ebira ancestors were of Jukun origin. According to this assertion, their ancestors left Wukari for Idah because of a dispute over the succession to their father's title. From the account given by Byng-Hall, "the Jukuns rose against their chief who later ran away with his followers and embarked on a journey to Apa.Here the history of the Ebira –Tao, as the people are normally called, from the context of their various struggles which are preserved in their traditions can be divided into four periods for the purpose of clarity.

The first period started in the Gongola Basin and ended with their migration to the lower Benue valley. According to tradition, the Ebira, in this period formed part and parcel of the Apa group (The Jukun) who founded the Kwararafa confederacy consisting of Pindiga, Kona and Kwararafa[6]. This was the time they were located in Ebira, a name they came to be known and identify themselves with.Reliable sources of their development during this period is very scanty. A date between 14th and 15th centuries is been suggested for the foundation of the three states that formed the Kwararafa confederacy namely Jukuns, Ebiras and Idomas but this date might not be realistic for the Ebira presence in this area [7]. This is because the Ebira tradition concerning this period says they were part of the movement that led to the founding of the Idoma Chiefdom. Infact, the Ebira trace their origin to the same source with Idoma. A 15th century visitor to the Idoma chiefdom talked of an already well- established society is the area[8].An Idoma tradition dates their migration from the Apa country to about 12th A.D. Even though there is not yet a strong basis for accepting this date, it is quite realistic in explaining the language diversification that has developed between the Jukun and the groups like the Ebira who claim affinity with them[9]. However, tentatively the date of between 12th and 14th centuries has suggested. This period is best described as Ebira pre-history as they had not yet become a distinct group from the rest of the Apa kingdom either in name or language.That distinction began to manifest in their migration from the Gongola basin to the lower Benue valley marking the second phase of the migration history.

The Ebira took their name in the lower Benue valley. Here they described themselves as people from "(E)bira"[10], where exactly they were located is not known but it can be argued that, from the traditions collected among Idoma that the Ebiras were already in the area of Agatu district when the Idoma ancestors met them. From there, the waves of migration dispersed the Ebiras and associated groups. Some moved towards western part (now Igala area) from where Okene and Igarra groups further migrated to Ebira Opete.In all these migrations the reason given is succession disputes, particularly when the head of the dynasty died since the parties regarded one another as equal partners as such eligible to lay claim to Attah dynasty. Sometimes, an out break of epidemic such as chicken pox could be responsible and, yet at another it could be an escape from punishment which the people considered unjustified and oppressive[11]. The dominant theme in the traditions of the people relating to their sojourn in Igala land is the role they played in the royal politics of Idah and the emergence of the Attah dynasty[12]. So, far no serious research has been conducted on this period of Ebira history. The of Ebiras settlement along the riverine area of Igalaland, the existence of many metropolitan Igala of Ebira derivation and the roles still reserved for officials of Ebira origin in the Atta kingship ritual, and above all, the very similarities in their cultural looks are enough indications that the claims of the Ebira in their tradition can be historically verified.

The third period in Ebira historical development started with their migration across the Niger at Etobe to the north bank of the Niger known as Ebira- Opete (old Ebira). The time of migration is said to be during the reign of the second Attah at Idah[13]. The reason given like the other is succession dispute in which they happened to be on the losing side. This reason might be dismissed on the ground of its stereo- typed nature which is common to all those groups who lay one claim or the other to Idah kingship. Such groups include also the Nupe and the various Idoma groups. The claim might not be far from the truth when it is realized that it is a common practice in the royal circle of Idah that the losing side in succession dispute is always obliged by tradition to move out of the capital en-mass to the hinterland of the kingdom and sometimes beyond the boundaries of the kingdom[14]. This was always used in the past to extend the influence of the Attah. The fact that the migration of the Ebira from Igala territory had a political cause is borne out of the fact that the dominant theme in the struggle of the early settlers of Ebira Okpete was how to secure political independence from the Attah in Idah. There was a gradual movement inland and spread North-west ward with some settling in Okehi and Upai hills and others in Igarra (otherwise known as Etuno).

An attempt to date the arrival of Ebira in their present place in colonial records suggested mid-18th century. Ibrahim, a pioneering scholar in Ebira history, has on the basis of generation succession and facts derived from colonial record and tradition from royal house of Igu, agreed with the mid-18th century date. The facts from Igarra traditions seem, to make this date too conservative. As noted above, the Ebira-Igarra tradition recorded two invasions of their territory by Benin forces during the reigns of Oba of Benin, Oba Akenzuwa (1661-1669) and Eroseyen (1935-1750).

Developments in Ebira-Opete and from there onwards can be assessed from the pattern of settlement in Okene-Eba. In Ebira-Opete they founded small settlement in or around Upake, Ochobanui, Ohuruku, Ohungwere, Egodo, Upaja Obangede etc. Some of these settlements have been named after former settlements or wards from which the people are said to have migrated. From Ebira- Opete the Ebira moved gradually in families, lineages and sometimes climbed to the hills of Okehi Upai and Eikoku, a compact area chosen for security purpose[15].Here they had such neighbours as Anowe (Okun Yoruba) Anuma, Ansoso, Anekpena, Anivasa (Bassa-Nge) with whom they interacted at various levels. Apart from marriage and trade links, the Ebira were sometimes in alliance and other times in conflict with these neighbours. The nature and tempo of relations were often determined by the interest at stake and influence by marriage ties.

These conflictual relationships sometimes resulted in communal wars among these neighbours making way for the expansion of Ebira settlement in the area[16]. The increase in the population of the Ebira in the new area overwhelmed their neighbours to the extent that they later had to give way. This assertion is supported by traditions that point that after the initial migration some clans who had earlier settled in Igala moved over to join their kith and kin in the Okene area[17].

The political organisation of the people in the new area reflected the settlement pattern which was based on family lineage and clan groups. The philosophy was also influenced by the fact that initially they had to move from Igala area and later Ebira- Opete to avoid the authoritarian rule of the Attah. Each clan group conducted its affairs as a semi autonomous entity. Even in each clan group lineage often acted independently. The power of lineage heads and clan chiefs was recognized in theory though in practice it was very ineffective. The only binding power of these officials derived from their religious role. These officials never failed to strengthen their political authority through religious sanctions which were thought to be ancestor ordained. The institutions such as ancestral cult featuring spirits like *eku-oba, ekuechichi, akatapa* and *eku-iraha* etc. were meant to give a political potency to the religious sanction in the hands of the authorities[18]. The religious sanction also ensured that minors, women, adolescents and people of servile origin conform to economic and political dictates of the head of households, the lineage heads and clan chiefs[19].

The Ebira land at the beginning of 20th century had a confederation of the five clan groups (Eika, Okehi Adavi, Okengwe and Ihima) each operating a divine form of government as established by Ododo of Okehi and Obaji of Eika (shrine), the two greatest heroes of Ebiraland. Following the social dislocation of the society and the break down of traditional law and order, wars, famine, series of interactions and intermingling with other people the two heroes enthroned the *Iregba* (shrine) as the institution of government and the masquerade as the instrument of discipline. Ododo and Obaji also established a divine form of chieftaincy. The installation of the Chief-Priest was linked with *Iregba* and the chief-elect had to pass through the ceremony of death and masquerade and was finally installed by the *ekuoba* (Masquerade).

Though the work of Ododo and Obaji was acknowledged throughout Ebiraland, each clan group was politically autonomous of the other. Each had its Chief-priest rotating among the clans in an established order of seniority. Complementing the work of the priest-chief was a gerontocracy made up of the council of elders. Depending on the fame or reputation and achievement of a Chief-priest, individuals from another clan group could take cases to him for solution, adjudication or settlement by oracle. This was the situation at the time the *Ajinomoh* (Jihadists) invaders arrived in the second half of the 19th century. The Ajinomoh war was the first to bring the Ebira together, unlike previous wars fought on clan basis, war leaders of various clan groups were compelled to take concerted actions and assist one another. The war was brought to an end through peaceful negotiation with the Ajinomoh by Ohindase Okomanyi Abogude at that time, the most famous of the chief-priests through his son-in-law and right hand man[21]. Atta Omadibi and other war leaders.The war led to the emergence of Okene as economically the leading town because their crops which laid to the east were safe while the crops of others were destroyed by the wars.

The existing socio-political organization was soon brought to question as a result of the religious development unfolding and spreading in the North. By the 1860s, the Jihadists based in Bida made their first incursion into Okene area by way of raiding. For the first time in their new country home, the Ebira were faced with a formidable enemy who could only be challenged through a united force under an able and acceptable leadership. This leadership was given by Ohindase Ukpai. The second incursion which came ten- years later, this time a combined force of Bida, Ilorin and Ibadan under Nupe leadership met a determined and united Ebira under the able leadership of Ohinadase Avogude[21].These two invasions had set the people on the way to central leadership and the Ohindase of Okengwe was assuming that role.

Developments in the post Ajinomoh (Jihadist) period which involved the whole Ebira always had the Ohindase acting on behalf of all the clan groups. For instance when Ebira-Igarras were engaged in war with Iboshi and the former needed the assistance of Ebira-Tao; they passed their request through the Ohindase. The Ohindase responded favourably by sending a contigent of Ebira war veterans drawn from all the clan groups[22]. Such was the picture in the Okene area up to the arrival of the British at the beginning of twentieth century. The British seemed to have recognized this fact initially when they accepted Ohindase's aid as their political agent. But they soon thwarted the process toward's centralized leadership by deciding to up-grade the office of a political agent over and above that of the Ohindase and other clan rulers.

The coming of British to the area in 1900 pushed the Ajinomoh invaders out of their operational headquarters in Kabba Division and set out to open up Ebira land.The British administration made some sweeping changes just to justify the recognition of Ibrahim Omadibi as the first nominal Chief of Ebira Division. These include the establishment of a judicial council in Okene having Omadibi himself as the chairman. This development invariably made him as central leader making other caretakers appointed by the British answerable to him. On the whole whether by accident or otherwise, this marked the beginning of a centralised administration in Ebiraland.

3.5 CENTRALIZED ADMINISTRATION IN EBIRALAND

The British applied the policy of indirect rule in Nigeria by making use of the existing institutions, which were less expensive in terms of finance and expatriate personnel. It was less likely to be resisted. In segmented societies with no central chiefs or dynasties, the policy created and imposed central leadership on them as it was better to rule through one central chief than through several chiefs. Having appointed Ibrahim on the ground of his brilliance and maternal connection with Atta Omadibi, whose title he took, they worked hard to justify his appointment, strengthened his seat and legitimized his position by making him to oversee the affairs of some communities placed under him. The colonial officers were so concerned with legitimitising the position of Atta Ibrahim that they made untenable claims. In 1923, the Resident of Kabba Province, during an official visit prepared a genealogical table for each of the leading chiefs in the Province in which Atta Ibrahim was shown as the 17th Atta in the dynastic line[23]. The Resident gave the history based on information collected locally, which showed that the Attaship of Ebira was senior to that of Igala. So Atta Ibrahim topped the chiefs' order of precedence. In fact, the concern to legitimize the Atta's position was so great that in 1922 the District Officers in charge of Kabba Division of which Ebira

District belong, held that the Atta was undoubtedly the highiest Priest and held the title of Ohindase[24].

Like the British colonial policy, Islam was a factor in the centralization policy. By the time the Jihad commenced by Uthman Dan Fodio in 1804 reached Ebira land in the 1860's, its spirit had degenerated into raiding for slaves and other forms of booty or tribute. Islam came to Ebiraland after the advent of the British through the return of ex-Ajinomoh captives and Hausa traders. The rapid growth of Islam in Ebiraland came through the Atta, first he got converted and secondly he went to Hajj. The idea of creating the emirate of Ebira under the Atta was raised by the Residents in 1923 but subsequently turned down by the Lt. Governor on the ground that the Atta was not Hausa[25].

However, religion rather than ethnicity should have been the determining factor. Spurred by the type of administration in the far north, the Atta appointed his brother, Yakubu as agent for Ihima in place of Opata who then 'disappeared,' an event that was to bring much trouble than the Atta had anticipated because his appointment was seen by many as an attempt to further perpetuate his oppressive rule and more importantly confirming the speculations that he had killed Opata (District Head of Ihima) to pave way for his younger brother.

Inspite of the formidable military power of the British, the forces against the centralized form of government were not easy to contend with. The traditional rivalry between Atta Omadibi and Agidi of Ukaka continued unabated. The opposition was such that Atta had to vacate his maternal relations' quarters at Okene Eba and set up his own (existing) place in Adavi land by 1929[26]. The factor of the new religion played its parts as it got linked with local politics. The Roman Catholic Mission (R.C.M) established in Ebira land back in 1913 was not making progress. Its leaders accused the Atta of favouring the Church Missionary Society (C.M.S), whose proprietor; Adebulu had been a tenant of Omadibi as against the sponsoring of Islam as a 'state' religion in Ebiraland. They won over Ozigizigi, who gave them his son (Abu) to be trained in the mission. They were determined to see Atta deposed and Ozigizigi installed as the central chief so that the Catholic religion could be sponsored as the 'state religion[27].

An even more fundamental opposition was constituted by the traditional forces. The appointment of Atta violated the traditional concept of leadership and chieftaincy in Ebiraland[26]. The weighty implications of the advent of the British were known to the people of Eika and Okehi but they had been advised during the annual examination of events at the *Iregba* on the futility of physical resistance, an advice some people of Okene and Iriku did not heed[28]. However, as the events unfolded, the people of Okehi and Eika began to ask some questions: that before the British came, each group had its *Iregba* and the strength of *Iregba* lied at Okehi and Eika; why should they now relocate it to Okene? Those who did not understand the role of the *Iregba* in governance and its subtle control over affairs would not appreciate the questions they raised. However the concerned people who were well aware of the implication of the relocation both politically and otherwise began to invoke clan sentiments to justify their claims.

3.6 PREVIOUS CONFLICTS IN EBIRALAND

Ebira land, unlike most societies in Africa, during and after colonization had series of experiences especially on issues relating to how resources, both tangible and intangible could be shared. In the process, conflicts ensued. The origins of some of these conflicts in Ebiraland have been properly documented.

3.6.1 OIVO ARIMOH CONFLICT.

There was a widespread forced labour and other related oppressive rule during Atta Ibrahim's reign. His mother was accused of maltreating young girls.Igbirra Native Authority File (I.N.A.) reported that:

"Gradually however, the Atta, drunk with power and feeling safe under the protective arm of the government, began to encroach upon th peoples right and to violate customs and traditions.This among other things led to 1924 uprising"[29].The introduction of aristocratic and feudalistic reforms by Atta provided a breeding ground for the crisis, moreso, the appointment of Alhaji Yakubu, his younger brother as the head of Ihima, the home of Arimoh greatly contributed.

Subsequent to that in 1924 when the resident captain of Lokoja, Byng Hall went on leave and Major Budgen came to act for him, Adamu *Arimoh* of Odosi, Ihima, who had witnessed the tax riots among the Egbas in 1918, while he was in the Abeokuta barracks, served as a soldier in the First World War and was discharged with honours, approached Major Budgen for appointment as a messenger/interpreter.The major was highly impressed with his credentials and without hesitation employed him. *Arimoh* who had earlier been jailed in 1922 for organizing resistance against Ogunmare had a pent-up hatred for the Atta over the appointment of the agent of Ihima and the disapperance of Opata.The resultant uprising led by Arimoh asking for Atta's removal is known as Oivo Arimoh crisis.[30]

3.6.2 OBANGEDE RIOTS OF MAY 7th, 1925.

For the Atta, the climax of the Oivo Arimoh crisis was yet to be over. Obangede people, for various reasons including their bitterness over their loss of what they considered their traditional leadership as well as the dignity of the land, refused to recognize the authority of the Atta and insisted that "if the Whiteman needed their taxes, he should come and collect it straight from their hands."[31]

However, the Resident insisted that the people must be made to acknowledge the authority of the Atta, and so, on 7th May, 1925, the Atta arrived with armed escorts to collect taxes[32].The people now joined by Aremoh's contingent from Ihima were engaged in a bloody battle with Atta's contigent.From the evidence gathered, it was so severe that Atta had to be smuggled out of the riot zone. However, some human and material losses were recorded on both sides.

3.7 IMMEDIATE CAUSES OF ABDICATION OF THE ATTA IN 1954

To many of the Atta's opponents, he could never go right whatever he did. The young and vibrant graduates of Roman Catholic Mission (R.C.M) in particular remained critical of his education policies. They felt bitter that the products of the Native Authority School (mostly Muslims) benefited more in the appointment to Native Authority Services. So when the Second World War broke out in 1939, many of them rushed to join the army. They returned emboldened to liken the Atta to Hitler against whom they had gone to fight. Traditional rivals like Ichimiri teamed up with them and seized advantage of the idea of democracy and constitutional changes being embarked on in the country to openly challenge him. They were supported by enlightened Ebiras resident in and out of Ebira land who as individuals had now one grudge or another with the Atta. Also the administration of Lokoja remained a thorn in the Atta's flesh. He had hoped to solve the problem of the town by posting his brother, Yakubu to Lokoja as the 'Wokili' but when the Atta was finally compelled to remove him and subsequently post him to Ajaokuta, a family feud ensued introducing a new dimension to his numerous problems.

The Ogori/Mangogo group in their part continued to petition the Atta and to agitate for a merger with western Nigeria. To also compound the situation, the traditional bedrock of Atta, the colonialists shifted their stand. All these problems combined to weaken the popularity of Atta and it manifested in 1954 Local Council Elections where Igbira Tribal Union (I.T.U) overwhelmingly won the polls. This automatically changed the structure, the sole Native Authority a Chief-in-Council changed to Chief and Council. The Atta found himself outvoted on many issues and he subsequently abdicated in 1954 to Idah, Kogi State.

[15]. Ibrahim Y. A., 'Politics in Ebira: The Centre and the Pheripheries', Ebira People Association Annual Lecture, Kano, 1979.

[16]. Ibid.

[17]. Amune, R.G.,'Peoples of the Niger River Benue Confluence', Ethnographic Survey, 1955.

[18]. Ohiare, J.A.,'Ebira History: Need For Proper Documentation' Ebira Peoples Assocation Annual Lecture, Zaria, 1981.

[19]. Ibrahim Y. A. 'The Coming of Central Administration in Igbira Division, I.S .A. Magazine, 1966.

[20]. Gazette of Nupe Province, NAK, 1920.

[21]. Interview with Mal. Ibrahim Y. A. on 18- 11 2004.

[22]. Interview with Ohindase of Okengwe, Chief Stephen S. on 21-12 2004.

[23]. Ibid.

[24]. Boston J.S., op. cit.

[25]. Interview with Chief Jimoh Ohiare on 21-10-2004.

[26]. Interview with Out of Ozumi, 21-12-2004.

[27]. Ibid.

[28]. Ibid.

[29]. Igbira Native Authority File, Law 27, NAK, 1925.

[30]. Interview with Obobanyi of Ihima, 22- 12-2004.

[31]. Ohiare J.A.,'Ebira History: Need for Proper Documentation', Ebira Peoples Association Annual Lecture, Zaria,1981.

[32] Ibid

ENDNOTES.

[1]. Sani, H. *The Rise and fall of State Governor in Nigeria. A case Study of Kogi State*, Desmon Tutu Press, Okene, 2003.

[2]. Ibrahim, Y.A.,'The Search for Leadership in a Nigerian Community: The Igbirra -Tao, C.1865-1954' *M. A. Thesis,* A.B.U.Zaria, 1968.

[3]. Interview with Chief S.Fache on 13 – 01- 2004.

[4]. Huxley, E, *Four Guineas: A Journey through the West Africa,* Macmillan, London,(1954). Also interview with Chief Audu, 21 -11 - 2004.

[5]. Interview with Mr, Joseph S. on 22- 11- 2004.

[6]. Aminu, J.S. *The History and culture of Ebira-Tao, Okene*, 2004.

[7]. Hamman M., 'The Rise and fall of the Emirate of Muri, 1812-1903', *Ph.D Thesis,* Ahmadu Bello University Zaria, 1963.

[8]. Gilmer E.R.,' Comments on Macleod's Report on the Igbira', NAK, 1926.

[9]. Palmer, H.M.,' The Jukun', NAK, 1923.

[10]. Erim, E. O., *The Idoma Nationality, 1600-1900: Problems in Studing the Origins and the Development of Ethnicity*, Enugu, 1981

[11]. Interview with Ohimege on 11-11- 2004.

[12]. Joseph Ukwedeh, *History of the Igala Kingom, C.1534-1854*, Arewa House Kaduna, 2003.

[13]. NAK 'Notes on Igbira History, 1921.

[14]. Boston J. C. 'The Igala Kingdom', NAK, 1968.

CHAPTER FOUR
POLITICS OF SUCCESSION IN EBIRALAND
4.1 INTRODUCTION

Irrespective of the forces that were against the adoption of a centralised traditional political system during colonial period, the system has come to stay. There is a general agreement among the people on the need to have a central leader that could articulate and aggregate their interests.However, where the problem still lies is the name of the title, the nature of the contest (mode of succession) and the roles that the various clans play in the selection/election of the paramount rulers.

As indicated in the previous chapters, there are five Districts namely Okengwe, Adavi, Eika, Okehi, and Ihima.Each of these Districts has a clanic structure.Some of these clans trace their ancestors to one source and also bear the same totemic values. This chapter discusses how the lack of consensus on the modality to be used and who is eligible to the throne have led to increase in clan consciouness and socio-political tension in Ebiraland.

4.2 ATTA AS A TRADITIONAL TITLE IN EBIRA LAND

The title 'Atta' has neither clear meaning nor origin in Ebira dialect. However, it means 'father' in Igala. The advent of 'Atta' institution into the political centre stage of the early Ebira community came about at the peak of the fierce contest of the Ozumiship by Ikunaye Aduhi of Idu lineage in Ogu clan in the 18Th century[1]. The vacuum created by death of the first Ozumi, Aroke Manti,prompted various group to indicate their interests in the stool. One of them was Omadibi Abanika, who hailed from Ede family of Ogu-clan, one of the sub clans excluded from Ozumiship. During his lifetime, according to oral history, Omadibi was well to do in all aspects of human endeavour and therefore wanted to use his well placed position to be installed as Ozumi, but he could not succeed."His consistent struggle and perseverance proved rewarding, when he discovered that he could lay claim to the Atta title then existing in one of the clans in Eganyi (in Ajaokuta) where his maternal grandfather was presiding over"[2]. There is an agreement among the elders in Ebiraland that Omadibi brought the title from Idah, in the present day Kogi State, but could not realise his dream of transforming it into a recognised chieftaincy title in Ebiraland before he died.

The death of Omadibi's grandfather amidst growing importance of chieftancy in Ebiraland rekindled the interest of Omadibi's maternal uncle and Omadibi's daughter. By the custom of Ebira, women could not participate in the contest yet Omadibi's mother was interested. So, the fight became a straight forward one between Omadibi's uncle and his mother[3]. Intense political intrigues and scheming soon began but Omadibi's mother won the heart and approval of the kingmakers in Ede family to shift the crown to her son. Omadibi was crowned as the Atta of *Ede* and decided to settle at Okoro- unne- Eba (now Okene). He was not recognised because of the strong presence of Ohindase (the most important title in Okengwe of which Okene was part of). The title of Ohindase was rotated among the four clans of Avi, Evini, Ovami and Omoye. From available records, Omadibi peacefully co-existed with Ohindase and gave him the respect; however, he was not able to develop the title into a full fledged traditional institution before he died[4].

The death of Ohindase, Pa Adano in 1917 created a power vacuum in Okengwe; this was the time colonialist needed somebody fairly literate, who could serve as an intermediary between them and the local people. By order of succession, Agada clan was to produce the next Ohindase, this did not materialize. Instead, the grandson of the late Omadibi, Ibrahim Onozuoira who had travelled far and wide and could communicate in English and Arabic caught the attention of the British. He emerged as the "Warrant" Chief of Ebira division. Although he was recognised by the British far above the other traditional title holders in the land, he was not allowed to bear the title of Ohindase. But for exigency reasons he needed a name by which he could easily be identified by both colonialist and the indigenous people. So, he preferred to be called (Atta) Ibrahim Onozuoira following the footsteps of his maternal grandfather. Othes argue that it was lack of consensus among the families in Agada clan to produce Ohindase that propelled the British to appoint Atta Ibrahim as representative of "Igbira"[5]. Ozigizigi was the consensus candidate favoured by the Okengwe kingmakers to occupy the throne but he could neither speak nor write in English. Attah Ibrahim Onuzuoira was not the popular choice of the people neither was the title (Atta) he eventually chose was generally accepted by the people. It was the colonialist who saw him as somebody already used to their values and taste therefore could go along way in ensuring their success in the area.

Despite the criticism levied against Attah Ibrahim, he ruled for 38 years. Throughout his reign there were several protests against him. Firstly, on the title, people especially his political opponents rejected the title saying it is alien to Ebira, and secondly, he was accused of inhumane attitude and insensitivity towards his subjects. By this period, people had shared a tendency toward establishing a central traditional institution but the name should reflect the culture and names of the Ebiras. This agitation came about the sametime with the agitation that the Anglicise version of spelling and pronouncing the name "Igbira" be changed to Ebira.

4.3 THE POLITICAL CIRCUMSTANCES FOR THE REPLACEMENT OF ATTA WITH OHINOYI

Igbira Tribal Union (I.T.U) led the rebellion against Atta Ibrahim.By which 1953 the union was controlling over 90% of the Native Authority[6]. This meant that the Union was enjoying the support from the grass roots that vehemently opposed Atta. Eventually, the Atta abdicated the throne in 1954. Series of recommendations were submitted to the Northern Regional colonial Government. Prominent among the submissions was the replacement of the title 'Atta' with that of Ohinoyi. In responding to their demand the Northern provincial annual report of 1956 stated that:

> ------- *in Igbira division on the 1st June 1956, Malam Muhammadu Sani Omolori has acceded, amidst almost universal acclamation, to the chieftaincy of Igbira, with the tittle of Ohinoyi, 23 months after the ex-Atta Alhaji Ibrahim had announced his intention to retire. The search "for a chief",was a most complicated exercise, along elaborated process of check and counter-check, bewildering to the peasant but justified in the result, the*

> *appointment of a chief who has the overwhelming support of the people. The appointment of a chief acted like a sedative on the Igbira-a volatile, lively and quick-tempered people7.*

The Igbira Tribal Union often times referred to the above quotation as the founding principle for the institutionalization of Ohinoyi as well as the recognised title of the paramount ruler of the land. The Northern Regional Government issued a public notice in the official Gazette on the appointment, and went to grade him as a head chief of the Ebira.

> *" ... It is notified for general information that His Excellency the Governor of the Northern region has been pleased to recognise Muhammadu Sani Omolori as chief of Igbira Tribe, with effect from 1st June 1956, and to grade him as a, Head Chief of the Second Class"8.*

This again explains and validates that Ohinoyi was properly appointed to represent Ebira not a "regent". While an indigenous traditional institution is being created carrying the name reflecting Ebira traditions, the installation of Ohinoyi created a division as a well as deep seated hatred among the Ebira people. In 1956, Native Authority Council wanted all families making up the clans in the whole area irrespective of political affiliation to send two representatives including the family Heads to give their respective views and decisons to the council[9]. The Igbira Native Authority was then made up of both Igbira Tribal Union (I.T.U) and Igbira Peoples Union (I.P.U) members with the former in overwhelming majority. The Igbira People Union did not recognise this arrangement and failed to attend the meetings held at various times to discuss the way forward. Most of the reformed proposals submitted by I.T.U were overwhelmingly endorsed, this gave them the opportunity to take absolute control of the affairs in Ebiraland.

There were high hopes among the Ebiras that the new era might bring the much desired change and openness in the administration of the land having Chief Sanni Omolori as the head of I.T.U and the Ohinoyi.

4.4　MODE OF SUCCESSION FROM ATTA TO OHINOYI

The administrative mode of governance of the Ebiras before the British was based on clan and age-grade system. The system had become a well entrenched and popularly accepted pattern of governing the people across the various settlements.

In the earlier system no single clan owed any form of central allegiance to any other clan. Law governing the conduct and behaviour of members of each clan is non conventional in nature, such laws were not written, they were passed on the injunctions of the early ancestors and deities called the "Ohiku"[10]. In most cases, the vacant position in any clan was filled via the consultation of oracle (eva). The Omadibis created the title of Atta for themselves therefore failed to spell out the modalities through which subsequent successors may emerge. The appointment of Ibrahim Onozuora was single-handedly done by colonialists. Similarly the procedures for successions were not properly identified. This is a total departure from what colonialist came to meet in Okengwe, the oldest district in Ebira land.

Groom had in 1904 recognised the existence of four (4) prominent sons in Okengwe among who the title of Ohindase would be rotated

> ... Oziyabi (Oziari) of the first branch was the first Ohindasi (Ohindasi), the second branch of the family supplied Okomain [Opkomanyi] as the second Ohindasi after which his successor will be found from the first branch again[11].

From the above, it is believed, according to oral tradition that, the paramount stool of Ohindase of Okengwe, then the most respected Chief would be rotated among the four sons of Okengwe. On this account, Groom is right going by the account given by Ohindase Steven Shaibu, who said that: "Oziovi was the first branch that produce the first Ohindasi, Okonmanyi Abogude was the second branch that supplied the second Ohindasi, Adano was the third, while the fourth Ohindasi was to be produced by Agada when Pa Adano died"[12]. Agada family, the fourth who was to produce Ohindase was denied the opportunity by the British. There is no historical account to suggest that the title of Ohindase was limited to only Ogu clan in Agada rather it belongs to the clans that make up the Agada and Okovi super clans. Again, the British did not take into consideration the established procedure by which the stool of Ohindase would be succeeded. On the whole, none of the traditional rulers across the district had any central recognition or an accepted mode of succession. The British was faced with two major problems because of this. Firstly, to accept one of the chiefs as a paramount chief and secondly, install a new title holder thereby creating a central chiefdom. It appears that British adopted the first method while it is to a large extent agreed among the people of Okengwe that Ohindase stool was, by tradition to be rotated among the four sons of Okengwe, it is however not documented that other districts had this kind of arrangement. As stated above, when Ohindase Arudi died in 1917, Atta Ibrahim was installed amidst protest.

Towards the end of 1953, the Igbirra Naitve Authority led by the I.T.U. having succumbed to the British innovation of central traditional institution, was anxious to have a central chief that would be appointed by the majority of Ebira. District assemblies were created for the purpose of selecting a head chief,and a series of consultations were held with representatives of clan leaders, after which Alhaji Muhammed Sani Omolori was dominated and eventually emerged as the sole candidate presented by I.T.U. This was subsequently approved by the Northern Regional government and appointed him as the Chief of Igbira on 1st June, 1959[13]. The appointment of "Ohinoyi" as the Chief of Igbira marked a radical departure from the existing status-quo because it abrogated the earlier "Atta of Igbirra"title. However, no clear procedures were laid down for the appointment of his successor, this was similar to the previous development where Atta Ibrahim was appointed by the colonialist because they felt it would be in their own to interest select him considering his qualities. As stated by Byng Hall they:

> *I have found him of great use in dealing with the Ebira, who also trust him, and have, to my knowledge refused bribes several times, and has been instrumental in bringing extortion cases and other intrigues to light. If you approve, am of the opinion that this would be the most satisfactory solution of the difficulties here[14].*

The "difficulties" stressed in Hall's report is, apparently, in connection with protests and grievances made against Atta Ibrahim prior to his appointment. In his annual report for 1917, Walker wrote:

> *As already reported they (British) unanimously chose Lerama (Atta Ibra) the grandson of the Ataru and son of the Ataru of Kukoroko. He had been previously brought to the notice of Mr Resident Ley Greaves by the late Ataru as being the most likely among the Ataru family to make a good District Head and was sent to be educated at Bida[15].*

From the above statement, it was only in the interest of the Omadibis that one of them, precisely, Ibrahim Onuzioira, be given the opportunity to serve his people. This is in sharp contrast to the view that Atta Ibrahim succeeded his grandfather as "the Atta of Igbira".

In another related argument Walker said:

> *"On the death of Omadibi, his daughter, (a woman of great personality and ability) managed to get her son Ibrahim (now Alhaji Ibrahim) recognized by*

Government though he had no rightful claim what so ever to the position[16].

The manner in which Alhaji Ibrahim Atta was installed generated a stiff opposition, especially among those who felt it was a total denial of their opportunity to produce the paramount chief. This category of people formed a group of opposition using the available means to bring his reign to disrepute in the form of uprising. Atta subdued several uprisings mainly from Ogu clan but also from leaders of the districts of Ihima, Okengwe and Eika who played prominent roles in these uprisings. In fears of persecutions most of them fled to the Southern part of the country but continued their struggle from there. The activities of the opposition groups both at home and away led to the formation of Igbira tribal Union (I.T.U) a group that played a very active role in the abdication of Atta in 1953. Throughout the period, I.T.U was advocating for the removal of Atta Ibrahim, it however, did not think about the mode of succession to the throne of Ohinoyi. This is an indication that I.T.U had allowed history and past mistakes to repeat itself. However, it could be argued that since Atta was the 'major obstacle' to the freedom of Ebiras, the desire to, at all cost, liberate the people preoccupied their minds as such the criteria for the appointment of the subsequent Ohinoyi were not in any way stated. Perhaps it was left to be discussed after the freedom had been achieved.

4.5 THE PROBLEM OF SUCCESSION OF THE OHINOYI.

With the death of the Ohinoyi Sani Omolori in 1996, the problem of succession became a burning issue. This was because the Ebira had no royal families for the paramountcy moreover, there was no acceptable method of selecting a candidate. Of the four paramount chiefs so far, three-(Atta Omadibi; Ohindase Arudi and Sani Omolori) had come from Okengwe, and one, Alhaji Ibrahim Onozuoiza, from Adavi. Indeed, before Atta Ibrahim, the Ebira had no central traditional leadership. In the case of Ohindase, if events were allowed to take their traditional course, Ozigizigi of Eire clan in Okengwe would have succeeded Ohindase Adano. However, such a succession arangement was not documented in any form, and thus, it was not legally binding on the Ebira at the time. It became obvious towards the end of 1996 that the Ebira might be heading towards a protracted conflict since it would be extremely difficult to have a consensus candidate to occupy the vacant stool. Aspirants emerged from all the Districts. Some of them even sponsored articles in newspapers in which they attemped to falsify history through the creation of non-existing dynasties. Others put forward spurious cases for the rotation of the stool, especially among the Districts of Ihima, Eika and Eganyi which had not in the past produced an Ohinoyi. It was in this state of uncertainty and conflict that the the Military Administrator of Kogi State, Col.B.L Afarkiriya, in 1997 constituted a seventeen man committee under the chairmanship of Mr A.E. Alieku to work out modalities for ascension to the throne of Ohinoyi of Ebiraland (see appendix A).In its report, the committee "by consensus", recommended the following order of rotation:

(i) Ihima (ii) Eika (iii) Eganiyi (iv) Adavi (v) Okengwe. Other recommendations were as follows:

(a) That this principle of rotation of paramount rulership in Ebiraland should permeate the clans in the districts.

(b) This rotation arrangement should become a permanent feature/ system of ascension to the throne of paramount stool of Ohinoyi of Ebiraland.

(c) Upon passing away of an Ohinoyi , the Ebira Area Council should meet immediately and elect an acting chairman of the council as Regent until a new Ohinoyi is appointed

(d) A candidate to be selected as the Ohinoyi of Ebira land shall among other things have the following attributes.

i. be a bonafide Ebira
ii. be not less than 50 years of age
iii. be healthy physically and mentally
iv. The candidate should belong to one of the religion recognised by the constitution of Federal Republic of Nigeria.
v. must reside in the official palace designated for the Ohinoyi
vi. The committee unaminously agree that the tittle 'Ohinoyi' of Ebiraland is the only acceptable title of the paramount stool[17].

In its Whitepaper on the report, the State Government accepted the recommendations and further emphasized that the stool of

Ohinoyi should be rotated only among the five traditional Districts of Ebiraland i.e Adavi, Okengwe, Ihima, Eika and Eganyi (see Appendix B).As soon as the government position became known, the Okehi District went to Court challenging their non involvement in the new rotational arrangement, by citing, among other things, the Groom report of 1909 which stated that the Ebira:

> On arrival in the new contry.... settled in 5 different districts of Okengwe, Odabi, Ihima, Ika and Okehi. These districts were formed by and took their names from the 5 sons of the man who was chief of the tribe when they were at Idah. His name was said to have been Igbira[18].

The Okehi District also buttressed their claim by citing evidence from historical artefacts and court rulings which were delivered in their favour but which both the Alieku report[19] and the government whitepaper[20] had ignored. On the other hand a cross section of the Ebiras opposed the inclusion of the Eganyi as one of the bonafide Districts in Ebiraland. They are largely regarded as having closer and historical ties with the Igalas. Thus, their inclusion in the rotation system was regarded by some as traceable to the influential role played by General Salihu Ibrahim (Rtd) as well as his closeness to the military Government[21].

On the 6th May, 1997, Ebira Traditional Council was given a copy of the white paper on the modalities for choosing the Ohinoyi of Ebiraland (see Appendix D). The council met on Friday 9th May 1997 to screen the aspirants and also close entries on the same day. Consequently, most candidates were not screened because it claimed that their applications were received late. This immediately sparked off violence across the land. In one of the cases, ten (10) lives were lost in one day and property worth million destroyed[22].

The protesters believed that the council refused to screen their candidates in order to pave way for a particular candidate. In all, 27 candidates applied and only three candidates were actually screened. (See Appendix C). As a result of the controversy surrounding the way and manner the council chairman handled the screening exercise; three of the members of the screening Committee boycotted the screening. At the end of exercise, Alhaji (Dr) Ado Ibrahim from Adavi District got six votes, Alhaji Ibrahim Sanni from Okengwe District got two (2) votes and Alhaji Yakubu A. Yusuf from Eika District had one vote.

The result thus gave Alhaji Adogu Ibrahim from Ehemi family of Aniku clan of Kuroko in Adavi Disrict the highest number of votes accordingly, in a letter of appointment dated 2nd June, 1999, the then Military Administrator, Col B.L Afakirya, contrary to the committee's recommendations, appointed him as the successor to the throne of Ohinoyi.

Shortly on assumption of office, the new Ohinoyi, Chief Ado Ibrahim, called a press conference. Many had hoped that he was going to take the opportunity to make attempts to heal the old wounds and reconcile with his rivals. Surprisingly, he stripped all the *Daudus* appointed by the late Ohinoyi of their titles. More importantly, he announced that he had now regained his ancestral seat and had therefore assumed the unofficial title of "Atta III" and was going to pay allegiance to the *Eheme* clan. Moreso, he publicly announced that "Ohinoyi is not a title, I am Atta, I must reign with the title and it is either I reign with the title or nothing else. Also, I must be addressed as His Royal Majesty"[23]. Consequently those affected by his pronouncement directly or indirectly instigated their supporters and thugs to publicly denounce the Ohinoyi on the grounds that they were fighting against domination and the imposition of an alien title.

Available documents have shown that Ado's father, Atta Ibrahim was referred to by the colonialists as 'Chief of Igbira', while his grand father, Omadibi Abanika, was never officially called Atta, but "Ataru"[24]. There was therefore neither Atta I nor Atta II. Consequently, Ado Ibrahim cannot enthrone himself as Atta the III. Those who applied for the Ohinoyiship and had their applications disqualified capitalised on this fact as well as the divisive utterances of the new Ohinoyi and went to court challenging the legality of his appointment. Subsequently, a High court at Egbe gave an injunction restraining the state government from presenting the Staff Office to the new Ohinoyi.

However, on September 18, 1999, the civilian Governor of Kogi state, Prince Abubakar Audu hurriedly and unceremoniously gave the Staff of Office to Ado Ibrahim, after the Egbe High Court had suspended its earlier injunction without given any reason, neither with the knowledge of the plantiff. The action of the state Governor is understandable especially when put within the context of the low level of support he got from Kogi central in the April 1999 General elections.Apparently, Prince Audu did that to neutralise the level of opposition in the Senatorial District. This move, however, did not yield the anticipated dividends because the Ohinoyi did not appear to enjoy the support of some of the elites that dominate the politics of Ebiraland.

There are several reasons which have been put forward for the Ohinoyi's apparent lack of popularity among the elites. One of this is said to be his style of leadership that is paying allegiance to a particular clan. Ado has ignored this by paying allegiance to *Idu* clan.Secondly, in the arrangement; Ohinoyi was to occupy the public palace jointly built by Ebira Division and the old Kwara state government in the 1970s. He has abandoned the palace and now operates from his private residence. Thirdly Ebira people had in the past unanimously agreed that unpopular title of 'Atta" should be abrogated in favour of a more indigenous such as Ohinoyi, this was further emphasized in Aileku's report and also reflected in the appointment letter given to him in 1997.

4.6   INSTITUTIONALISATION OF OHINOYI AND THE TRANSFORMATION OF CLAN CONFLICTS

The attempts at centralising and possibly closing the democratic space for the traditional stool started when Atta Ibrahim Onozuioza was the Chief of Ebiraland.Some of the people he installed as clan heads contravened the then exiting traditional practices. For instance he appointed Chief Agidi from *Eire* clan as the fourth Ohindase. This ignited conflict because the *Eire* clan was not among the four clans that could originally lay claim to Ohindaseship[25]. On the other hand, the *Eire* people seized the opportunity to rewrite history in their favour by establishing that they had in the past occupy the throne of *Ohindase*, and as such gaven total support and allegiance to Atta Ibrahim.

Similarly, Ohinoyi Sani Omolori had in his capacity attempted to build his own empire by restructuring the traditional institution. For instance, he initiated some chieftaincy titles and conferred them on some of his loyalists. While the primary aim might be to recognise their contributions to the development of the land, it was also intended to seek for their support for Ohinoyi and his plans. It is obvious therefore, that the Ohinoyis have been in favour of a hierarchical traditional institution having them on the top, to be followed closely by their District appointees even as many clan leaders and elites are edged out.

Under Ohinoyi Ado Ibrahim, some purpoted reforms were undertaken, which were like the previous ones resulted in centralising and limiting the level of participation of the public, especially the elites. While some, particularly those that benefitted or stood to benefit from the reform saw nothing wrong with whatever the Ohinoyi did, other expressed reservations and fears that the intended goals when achieved, might bring about their total exclusion and alienation in the running of the affairs of the traditional institution or even prevent the interested persons among them from becoming Ohinoyi in the foreseeable future.

Considering the increasing roles played by the traditional chiefs as a result of the recognition accorded them by the state, the affected elites who wanted to use the institution as an avenue to get their political goals realised were at the risk of missing out. For instance, Chief A.T. Ahmed, Chief Ohida, Mal. Ohize, Senator Mohammed Ohiare, Dr John Lawal, Air Comodore. Hamza(Rtd), Alhaji Badamasau, just to mention a few were the group of people with vested clan interests groomed by the late Ohinoyi Sani Omolori to play active roles both in political and traditional matters affecting Ebiraland. Incidentally, they were among the notable men recognised and conferred with, various Chieftaincy titles by the late

Ohinoyi but got relieved of the titles by present Ohinoyi. This development was seen by them as a slap on the traditional institution and also an attempt to circumscribe their activities in Ebiraland.

What appears to be a consensus amongst these people was that there was no longer a traditional leader whose voice can be heard and respected by the people. Senator Mohammed Ohiare expresses this position:

> *What is still amazing, so baffling about the entire sordid situation is that we have been finding it hard to unravel the mystery behind the cause of the recurring bad omen.On the whole, it is the lack of political and traditional leadership. Unlike the Atta of Igala whose views in many situation are usually respected and adhered to by the igala people the people of Ebira do not listen to the Ohinoyi neither do they respect his views.*[26]

Some believe that the royal father has got himself entangled with series of things that do not befit his status. Many are of the opinion that the Ohinoyi is not respected because his installation was not done in the proper way as it was masterminded by the military regime.Others believe that he bought his way to the throne. Most of the times he pursued personal vendetta, capitalizing on minor issue to hit back at his real and perceived opponents. The recent political conflict in Ebira land was said to be caused by A.T Ahmed and his supporters[27]. He has over 1600 well armed thugs across the land. Guns are freely given to them with the instruction to unleash harvoc on any of the Ohinoyi's loyalists. Most of the notorious Idoji boys are on his payroll[28].

Alhaji Salihu Ohize the incumbent chairman of Okene local Government Council is one of the strong supporters of Senator Ahmed and has effective grip on the Youth of the land. He denied the allegation that he armed most of the youth in Idoji. In his own words:

".....the truth is that Kogi Central is a highly populated part of the state but we have no land and we have a very large population of unemployed youth. We knew that unemployment is a big problem all over the country but the situation in Ebiraland has become overwhelming. Lack of employment has made the youth who are prone to manipulation, to be easy target by politicians who use them to cause trouble".[29]

He further maintained that,"normally an African man respects the opinion of the traditional rulers no matter their political leaning or religious affiliation. But what we have in Ebira land is not only that people do not accept Alhaji Ado Ibrahim as Ohinoyi but also he is not playing the fatherly role he is expected to play during crisis situations.......calling the Ohinoyi to order" [30].

Chief Ohida was more direct in his attack of the on going reform of the traditional institution by Ado Ibrahim "the implication of him (Ado) being addressed as his royal majesty is that all the Ebira sons and daughters are his subjects not having equal rights as his family members".[31] One thing is common to these arguments, traditional issues should be opened to all to participate and that a traditional leader should be as modest, neutral and a uniting symbol as possible.

While most people claim that the conflicts in Ebira are as a result of the power tussle between Ohinoyi and his supporters on one hand, and Senator A.T Ahmed on the other, others believe that the current conflicts in Ebira have spiritual dimension. Prominent among those with this belief is Mal. Ismaila (an Islamic Leader); he is of the opinion that Ebira is under a curse from the past; when Adamu Atta was the governor of Old Kwara state "as a result of the political rift between him (Atta) and Dr Saraki who influenced the election of Adamu Atta as Governor of Kwara State, political thugs went to Ilorin and chased out notable indigenes of the town from Ilorin township stadium with some vicious and stern looking masquerades. It is believed that the people used the Koran to place a curse on Ebiraland.[32] The opinion of Mal Ismaila and other people who witnessed the scene in 1982 is that the curse is largely responsible for the series of violence in the land.

Some traditionalists tend to disagree with the above assertion; instead they located the genesis of the crisis within Ebiraland. The Otu of Okene Mr Teacher Benedict, Mal Sani, the custodian of "Oratauvo" masquerade, Asema of Adavi, Mal Maiyaki, and Chief Sani Enesi, a herbalist, all believe that the crises are as a result of the 'total disregard' of the traditional values and obligations by half baked Muslim fundamentalists. They are of the view that the fundamentalists are hell bent on destroying the traditional beliefs our ancestors bequeathed to us. In those days during the festival period, people from Britain and U.S.A. could freely come and enjoy the festival.[33] The very moment these fundamentalist started disgracing and even slaughtering masquerades in public, we started experiencing the crisis. These groups of people are of the opinion that the god is angry with the land. "We have defiled the sacred shrines of our ancestors hence, the ancestors are angry with the land".[34]

Similar to the above belief of the traditionalists is the opinions of some Christian leaders in Ebirland. Bishop Herbert Haruna, Pastor Joseph Suleiman of the Redeemed Christian Church of God, Rev Adomu and Rev Father Oniade of Christ the king Catholic Church attribute the cause to the fact that the land is under satanic influence.

In the words of Mr Joseph Suleiman: "You can't imagine a young boy telling people that he is out to kill more people to equal the record of his rivals".[35] "Human blood is like water before these boys, they are always eager to kill".[36] Rev. Amedari is of the opinion that:

> *The problem with Ebira land is spiritual, day in day out we witness crises of different dimension, one amazing thing is that sometime the immediate cause of the problem cannot be investigated. When one assesses this problem, you will find out that it is really a spiritual case. It is against this background that, Christian Association of Nigeria Kogi State chapter in general and Ebira branch in particular decided to invite the renowned German evangelist. Reinhard Bonke to Okene with the view to delivering the land from the hand of satanic forces"*[37].

There is an agreement among the people on the issue; they all believe that there are conflicts manifesting themselves in the form of clan and communal disturbances. They only differ in their cognition and the origin of the conflicts. Religion in Africa has become a veritable means of mobilisation and a refuge from destruction, in terms of conflicts this makes easier for the various religious leaders to look for converts which in turn develop the faith. To an extent, religion can reframe the mindsets of people to shun violence but has limitations in tracing the origins of certain conflicts in historical terms as in the case of Ebiraland, neither does it adequately provide explanations on the rationale behind the reforms.

END NOTES

[1]. Interview with Ohindase, Chief Bello Stephen on 11- 11- 2004.

[2]. Ahmadu E.D. *Who Are the Ebiras*?
Beth Bekka, Maiduguri, 2004.

[3]. Interview with Ohindase, Chief Bello Stephen on 11-11- 2004.

[4]. Ibrahim Y.A.'Politics in Ebiraland: The Centre and The Peripheries', Ebira Peoples Association Annual Lecture, Kano, 1979.

[5]. Interview with Chief Emmanual Ozigi on 12-12- 2004.

[6]. Ahmadu E.D. *Who Are the Ebiras*? Beth Bekka, Maiduguri, 2004.

[7] Ibid

[8]. Northern Regional Notice, 1956.

[9]. Interview with Ohindase, Chief Bello Stephen on 11-11- 2004.

[10]. Sani H. *Panoramic View of Chieftaincy Titles in Nigeria*. Desmon Tutu Press, 1998.

[11]. Groom, A. 'Schemes for the consolidation of the Igbiras from' N. A. K Documentation, 1909.

[12]. Interview with Ohindase, Chief Bello Stephen on 11-11- 2004.

[13]. Northern Regional Gazette No.27, 1956.

[14].Lokoja Provincial File; No. 2668, NAK, 1917.

15]. Ibid.

[16].Ibid.

[17]. *Ebiconews*, June 19TH, 1997 Vol.14. No 2.

[18]. Groom, A. 'Schemes for the consolidation of the Igbiras from' N. A .K Documentation, 1909.

[19]. *Ebiconews*, June 19TH, 1997 Vol.14. No 2.

[20]. Ibid.

[21]. Interview with Mal. Samaila on 12 – 12 – 2004.

[22]. ***Ebiconews***, June 19TH, 1997 Vol.14. No 2.

[23].The Democract 18 – 3 – 1997.

[24]. Ahmadu E.D. ***Who Are the Ebiras***? Beth Bekka, Maiduguri, 2004.

[25] Ibid

[26]. Interview with Senator Mohammed Ohiare on 10 – 11- 2004. Okene

[27] Field Observation

[28] Ibid

[29]. Interview with Mal. Salihu Ohize.

[30]. Ibid.

[31]. Ohida, Ibrahim. ***Ebira at Political Cross-Roads: The Way Out,*** Segmak, Ilorin, 2002.

[32]. Interview with Mal. Samaila on 12 – 12 – 2004.

[33]. Interview with Otu of Ozumi on 23 – 12 - 2004.

[34]. Interview with Mal. Sani on 24 – 12 -2004

[35]. Interview with Mr. Suleiman Joseph on 10 – 11- 2004.

[36]. Ibid.

[37]. Interview with Rev. Adomu on 12 – 12 – 2004.

CHAPTER FIVE
SUMMARY, CONCLUSION AND RECOMMENDATIONS

5.1   SUMMARY:

Attempts have been made to establish how traditional institutions and clan sentiments shape the socio-political relations in Ebiraland. In chapter one, we discussed foundational problems in which traditional institutions and beliefs impact on the communal conflicts that are rampant in the area, the research proposition, the rationale behind the research undertaking, methodology (both primary and secondary sources) and definition of concepts. The entire work is within the theoretical analysis of environmentally indueced and Elite theories.

In chapter two we appraised several literatures considered to be relevant to the study of conflict. In this chapter, it has been discovered that there is a general consensus among scholars in the field of conflict, that conflict is inevitable in human organisation, however, some of the conflicts can take political dimension and with political motivation. Also, conflict can arise as a result of perceived incompatibility over material or symbolic issues such as resources and other societal benefits. It could also be as a result of the differences in terms of goals, values, system and the interests at stake. Several issues are involved in conflict; these include: identity, governance and resources (tangible and intangible). Since conflict is seen as an evitable phenomenon, it is therefore, imperative to discuss the mechanism through which it can adequately be managed (conflicts resolution). We have discovered that conflict is dynamic, its causes and the dimensions it can take depends on the situation and the given circumstances.

In Africa, some conflicts are as a result of chieftaincy titles. It can occur in any society whether heterogeneous or homogenous, developed or developing countries.

In chapter three, we attempted to trace the evolution of Kogi state the political importance of Ebira in the state. We described the vegetation of state, ethnic composition, population and the number of local government councils that make up the state. It is also discussed that the origin of Ebira as an ethnic group is contentious, there are various explanations or theories that attempt to explain the origin of Ebira; there is Ebira-Igala consanguinity theory, Ebira-Jukun consanguinity theory, and the establishment of Idah Dynasty. Despite the controversy, it is been found during the course of the research that the Ebiras started their journey from the Gongola Basin and ended it with their migration to Lower Benue Valley. They, within this period, formed part and parcel of the Apa group (the Jukuns) who founded the Kwararafa confederacy consisting of Pindinga, Kona and Kwafararafa. Because of certain transformation and increasing quest for the establishment of independent political institution, Ebiras had to migrate from several places before they finally settled down in their present home country. Historical evidence has shown that Ebiras lived together in clans and sub-clans and one could easily guess the clans areas or settlements from the particular locality.

In chapter four we have discovered that over the past two decades, conflicts in Ebiraland, often rooted in traditional disputes, have been compounded by accelerated economic, social and political transformations. These developments have spurred communities and districts to look for new ways to address long standing problems of poverty, inequality, and injustice. At the sametime, rising popular expectations, increasing competition over resources and opportunities, and sharpening perceptions of inequality and injustice are leading to increased tensions and in some instances violent conflicts.

5.2 CONCLUSION

The study has revealed that the inability of the Ebira traditional institution and the associated groups to work out an aggeeable mode of succeession to the paramount stool of Ohinoyi especially on how people from the various Districts could access the throne has negatively impacted on the conflicts.

Secondly, the study has found out that Ohinoyi is regarded as the most prominent traditional chief by the Ebira people however; he does not enjoy the needed influence and authority over the clan heads/leaders. Inotherwords, while there is hierarchy at the level of Ohinoyi, there is nothing of such at the Districts. This lack of uniformity often times lead to clash of personality between Ohinoyi and clan leaders on one hand, and elites from the Districts on the other.

Lastly, the geographical nature of Ebiraland is such that there is litle or insufficient land when compare to rapid increase in population of the area. Land tenure system of land holding still exists with clan heads overseeing the distribution of the lands in their dormains. Most times clan affliation is the major critarium for having access to land. Elites and clan leaders do invoke clannish sentiments in defence of the autonomy of their clans and against the reforms that they perceive as a ploy to reduce the power they exercise over the land.

5.3 RECOMMENDATIONS

Based on historial facts, Ebiras had no central traditional political leadership, but with the modern challenges and emphasis on leadership, it is possible and rational to have a central chief, therefore, the stool of Ohinoyi that appears to have brought about disagreements among the districts. The only practical alternative is the modification of the method proposed by Kogi State government stating that; the Central political leadership of Ohinoyi should be rotated among the five district (or sons of) of Ebira namely; Eika, Okengwe, Adavi, Okehi and Ihima (in order of seniority). But each of the major branches is now claiming seniority without substance. Therefore, the rotation order should be by alphabetical order, ie (1) Adavi, Eika, Ihima Okehi and Okengwe. In addition, since these districts are deeply segmented along clans it will be unrealistic not to include clan as one of the criteria. Therefore, while the stool is rotated among the recognised districts, in each district, the order of seniority of the clans should be taken into recognition for the fact that there is a general consensus among the cross section of Ebiras concerning the clan seniority in all the districts.

Government should revisit the up-grading it hurriedly did in 1991. Preferably, if possible, the upgrading should be reversed to their former status. On the alternative, the following criteria should be religiously and consistently used for up-grading of Ebira traditional Chiefs:

i. functions performed in Pre-British Ebiraland
ii. number of clans or families or kindred ruled or the population of clans\families ruled.

Also Local Government Traditional Council should be abolished and all the benefits acruable to them be stopped immediately since it has aggravated the clan conflicts.

Kogi State government should make an official declaration compelling Ohinoyi of Ebiraland, Alhaji Ado Ibrahim to relocate from his personal house to the government owned palace specifically built to house Ohinoyi and his household. On a more serious note, government must carry out a comprehensive renovation work on the public palace to befit his taste and position.

In all ramifications, marriage institution in Ebira land has collapsed. Most married men and women do not look at marriage as a union in which the two parties mutually involved respect the dignities of each other. Most men perceive it as a mere union to produce children after which the women are totally neglected. In most cases, the children of the abandoned women neither get adequate attentions from their mothers nor fathers. Special public orientation programes should be organised by the State and Local governments within the Senatorial District to educate the people on the short and long term effects of breaking marital vows. Government should arrest and prosecute the "irresponsible politicians" who are fond of deceiving young girls into marriage only to abandon them sooner or later.

Notable politicians are usually indicted in most of the communal disturbances but government does nothing in calling them to order. Those politicians who have resorted to training political thugs and clan militia groups whom they consider as useful tools in achieving their selfish interests should be blacklisted (by barring them from contesting for any public office for special number of years) and be made to sign an agreement that will ensure peace and tranquillity in their domains.

Inter-clan and districts conferences should be organised on regular basis to discuss ways and means of resolving disputes in the area as well as to aquaint them with latest efforts been made by the government and the leaders of thought from Ebiraland in this direction.

There is high rate of 'drop-out' among the youths in the area. Reasons could be found within the context of the general economic hardship in the country.Some of these young boys and girls have potentials to become great leaders of tomorrow, what they need is just encouragement and support,both financially and morally.Local governments should reorganise and re-orientate the poverty alleviation scheme that for now only cater for the political thugs recruited by the council chairmen to serve as their security men, to cover the determined youths but without empowerment. If this is done, it has the propensity to change the mindsets of the people of Ebiralnd particularly, the young ones toward violence.

END NOTES.

1. Dunmoye, A. 'General Survey of Conflicts in the Middle Belt zone of Nigeria', In: **Survey of Conflict in Nigeria, Journal of Centre for Peace Research and Conflict Resolution**, National war college Abuja, 2003.

SELECTED BIBLIOGRAPHY

BOOKS

Arthur, Wisting, *Global Resources and International Conflicts*, Oxford University Press: London, 1994.

Chabal, Patrick,, *Power in Africa, An Essay in Political Interpretations,* St Martins Press: New York,1992.

Coser Lewis, *The Function of Social Conflicts*, Free Press: New York.1995.

Dauda, Ahmadu, E.*Who are the Ebiras?* Beth Bekka: Maiduguri, 2004.

Eghosa Osaghae, *Ethnicity, Class and the Struggle for State Power in Liberia*, CODESRIA : Dakar, 1998.

Ekeh Peter, Ekeh. 'Citizenship and Political Conflicts: A Sociological nterpretation of the Nigerian Crisis', In: Okpaku(ed), *Nigeria:* **Dilemmas of Nationhood,**Third Press: New York,1977.

Follet Parper, *Dynamic Administration,*Harper: New York,1992.

Harry Miall, *The Peacemakers: Peaceful Settlement of Disputes,* Macmillan: London, 1992.

Harowtz Donald, **Ethnic Group in Conflicts**, University of California Press: Bekeley, 1985.

James Himes .S, **Conflicts and Conflicts Management**, University of Georgia Press: Athens,1980.

Jega, Attahiru, (ed), **Identity Transformation and Identity Pollitics Under Structural Adjustment in Nigeria** ,Nordiska: Uppsala,1996.

Keating, Michael , **Nations Against the State: The New Politics of Nationalism in Qubec and Catalonia**, St.Martin's: New York,1996.

Linchwe ii,(Chief),'The Role a Chief can Play in Botswana's Democracy, In: Holm, J. and Molutsi, P.(eds),**Democracy in Botswana**, Macmillan: Gaborone,1989.

Mamdani Mahmud, **Citizen and Subject: Contemporary Africa and The Legacy of Late Colonialism**, David Philip: Cape-Town, 1996.

Merw, Vander. ,**The Truth and Reconciliation Commission and Community Reconciliation: An Analysis of Competing Strategies and Conceptualisation**, Manchester University press: Manchester, 2003.

Neiburg, Benjamin. *National Self-determination in Post-Colonial Africa*, Lynn-Reiner:Boulder 1985.

Nnoli, O. (ed), *Ethnic Conflicts in Africa,* CODESRIA: Dakar, 1998.

Ohida, Ibrahim, *Ebira at Political Cross-Roads: The Way Out*, Segmak Ltd: Ilorin, 2003.

Otite, Onigwu, *Ethnic Pluralism and Ethnicity in Nigeria,* Shaneson: Ibadan,1990.

Sani, Habibu A. , *Sociology of the Ebira-Tao People of Nigeria*, Desmond Tutu Press: Okene, 1993.

Sani, Habibu A., *Panoramic View of Chieftancy Titles in Nigeria* Desmond Tutu Press; Okene, 1998.

Stuart, Hall 'Ethnicity, Identity, and Difference' In: Geoff and Sunny, (eds), *Becoming National,* Reader: New York, 2001.

Suliman, Mohammed, (ed) , *Ecology, Politics and Violent Conflicts,* Zed Books: London, 1998.

Swingewood, Allan, *Marx and Mordern Social Theory*, Macmillan: London, 1975.

Ukwede, Joseph. , *History of the Igala Kingdom (1534-1854)*, Ahmadu Bello University Press: Zaria, 2003.

JOURNAL ARTICLES

Bangura, Yusuf. ,'Intellectuals,Economic Reforms and Social Change:Constraints and Opportunities in the Formation of a Nigerian Technology', In: *Journal of Development and Change*, Vol.25.No.2, 1994.

Bartos,O.J,'Modelling Distributive and Integrative Negotiations'. In: *Annals*.Vol.52.No.1, 1995.

Berman,B.,'Ethnicity,Patronage and the African Elites:The Politics of Uncivil,' In: *Afriacan Affairs*, Vol.97.No.43,1998.

Comaroff, J.L. ,'Rules and Rulers: Political Processes in Tswana Chiefdom'. In: *Man* (N.S).Vol.13.No.45,1979.

Eyoh, David'Through the Prism of a Local Tragedy:Political Liberalisation and Elite Struggles for Power in Camerooon, In: *Africa*, Vol.68.No.3,1998.

James, Demers. ,'Settling International Disputes'. In: *Management*.Vol.21No.3.2002.

Kwame, Arthur B.,'Chieftancy and Politics in Ghana Since 1982. In: *West African Review*, Vol, 31, 2001.

Lemarchand, R 'Genocide in the Great Lake: Which Genocide? Whose Genocide? In: *African Studies Review*.Vol.41.No1.1998.

Pareto, Vilfredo, 'The Mind and Society,'
In: **Livingstone** *Journal*, Vol.4 No 45, 1939

Siever, Harneit A.,'Igbo Tradinational Rulers;Chieftancy and the State in Southeasern Nigeria'.In:***African spectrum,***Vol.33.No2,1996.

Smith, Z.K, 'The impact of Political Liberalization and Democration on Ethnic Conflict in Africa;An Emperical Test of Common Assumptions'.In: ***Journal of Mordern African Studies***. Vol. 38, 2002.

Thomas, Homer-Dixon.,'On the Threshold,Environmental Changes and Acute Conflicts'.In:***International Security.***Vol.16 No.3,1994.

Thomas, Homer-Dixon,,'Environmental Scarcity and Violence; Evidence from Cases.In: ***International Security***, Vol.19.No.4,1994.

Warnier, J.P,,'The King as a Container in th Cameroon'.
In: ***Paideuma***.Vol.No.39,1993.

REPORTS

Human Rights Watch,'Playing the Communal, Land Communal Violence and Human Right, New York.1995

U.N.D.P 'Deepening Democracy in a Fragmented World. In: *Human Development Report.*New York.2002

NATIONAL ARCHIVES, KADUNA

NAK, Lokoprof, 37/1922, Kabba Province Annual Report by F.F.W.Byng-Hall

NAK, Lokoprof, 216/1922, Pagan Priest Appoinment to Chieftainships

NAK, SNP142P/1917, Re-assessment Report, Pategi District, Historical Notes on Nupe.

NAK, K2445, Idoma: The Resident of Kabba Province, 1927.

NAK, K5523, Igbira: The Resident of Kabba Province, 1956.

NAK, Lokoprof.296, Notes on Igbira History.

UNPUBLISHED WORKS

Ibrahim, Y.A., (1962),"The Seach for Leadership in a Nigerian Community:The Igbira-Tao,C.1865-1954",M.A.Thesis, A.B.U.,Zaria,

NEWSPAPER

Daily Times, December 6th, 1955.(Vol.92 No.21) Lagos.

Ebiconews, June 10th 1994.(Vol.14 No.56) Kaduna.

West African Pilot, January 25th, 1956 (Vol.) Lagos.

INTERVIEWS

Interview on 8 / 8 / 2004, with Senator Mohammed, Ohiare, Okene.

Interview on 8 / 8 / 2004, with Mal.Ohize Salihu. Okene Local Government Chairman, Okene.

Interview on 13/8/2004, with Mal.Ismaila Yakubu.An Islamic Scholar, Okene.

Interview on 14 / 8 /2004, with Chief Ben. (Teacher). Otu of Okene.

Interview on 15 / 8 /2004, with Pastor Joseph Suleiman, President General, Ebira Youth Congress, Okene.

Interview on 15 / 8 / 2004 with Chief Onimisi Joseph, Otaru of Ohiongwa, Ihima.

Interview on 10 / 10 / 2004, with Dr. Habibu Angulu Sani, Okene.

Interview on 11 / 10 / 2004, with C hief Siyaka Okaraga, Obobanyi of Ihima.

Interview on 13 / 10 / 2004 with Otaru of Ure, Ihima.

Interview on 01 / 11/ 2004 with Chief Stephen S. Ohindase of Okengwe

Interview on 24 / 12 / 2004 with Mal.Ibrahim Sadiku, Asema of Adavi., Adavi-Eba

APPENDIX A

MEMBERS OF THE COMMITTEE SET-UP TO WORK OUT THE MODALITIES FOR THE APPOINTMENT OF THE NEW OHINOYI

S/NO	NAME	DESIGNATION	AREA
1.	Mr. A.E. Aileku	Chairman	-
2.	Dr. A. Tom Adaba	Member	Adavi
3.	Engr. Y.A. Moru	Member	Adavi
4.	Mal. Mohammed I Bello	Member	Adavi
5.	Hon. Y. I. Amoka	Member	Okengwen
6.	Alh. M. Kokori Abdul	Member	Okengwen
7.	Alh. Sule Aliu	Member	Okengwen
8.	Mr. Z. A. O. Bello	Member	Ihima
9.	Hon. Yakubu O. Ogido	Member	Ihima
10.	Mr. Samuel A. Sule	Member	Eika
11.	Alh. M.J.A. Ajanah	Member	Eika
12.	Hon. Salawu Atimah	Member	Eika
13.	Alh. Mamudu Akaba	Member	Eika
14	Alh. M.K.A. Ibrahim	Member	Eganyi
15.	Mal. Saka Ibrahim Abu	Member	Eika

16.	Alh. Abdul-Aziz O. Abu	Member	Eganyi
17.	Alh. A.K. Mohammed	ecretary	Eganyi

Source: GHLK/KGS/28/AD of June, 1997.

APPENDIX B
KOGI STATE GOVERNMENT OF NIGERIA PROCEDURE FOR ASCENSION OF THE THRONE OF OHINOYI OF EBIRALAND EDICT, 1997

The military Administrator of Kogi State of Nigeria, Col. B. L. Afakirya hereby makes the following Edict:

1. This Edict shall be known as procedure for ascension to the throne of Ohinoyi of Ebiraland Edict (No. 3 of 1997 and shall be deemed to have come into force on the 6th day of May 1997.
2. The stool of the paramount ruler of Ebiraland who shall be known as Ohinoyi is here by established.
3a. Ascension to the throne of Ohinoyi of Ebiraland wherever it is vacant shall be by rotation the five (5) traditional district of Ebiraland Ohinoyi.
b. For avoidance of doubt the five (5) traditional districts in Ebiraland are, Adavi, Okengwe, Ihima, Eika and Eganyi.
c. All eligible and interested sons of Ebiraland are free to contest for the stool of Ohinoyi of Ebiraland under this arrangement provided that, any District that has taken its turn in this rotational order shall not take part until it comes to its turn.
4. Ebira Area Traditional council shall remain the council of kingmakers.
5. the functions of the council king makers shall be as follows:
a. To announce the passing away of an incumbent after consultation with the family of the Ohinoyi and the Kogi State Governments, such announcements must conform to the existing and recognised tradition of Ebira people.

b. To meet immediately upon the vacancy of the throne of Ohinoyi of Ebiraland and elect an acting Chairman of the Council as regent until the new Ohinoyi is appointed.

c. To set in motion machinery for appointment of a new Ohinoyi immediately the stool becomes vacant.

d. To receive applications from eligible and interested sons of Ebiraland for consideration.

6. During the period of selection of a new Ohinoyi

a. There shall be no masquerade outing or public procession rallies.

b. There shall be no open campaign for or against any interested candidate.

c. Any person who contravenes section 6a and 6b above is quilty of an offence and shall be liable to imprisonment for three years without an option of fine.

7. No appointment of an Ohinoyi of Ebiraland shall be valid until the Chief Executive of the state has approved such appointment.

8. No provisions of any law of the state that is in force shall invalidate the provision of this Edict.

Source: Made at Lokoja 6th day of May, 1997.

APPENDIX C
NAMES OF THE CANDIDATES FOR THE OHINOYI STOOL AFTER THE DEATH OF OHINOYI MUHAMMADU SANI OMOLORI

S/N	NAME OF ASPIRANT	DISTRIC/AREA
1	Alhaji (Dr) Abdulrahaman Okene	Adavi
2	Dr. Abdulmumuni Atta	Adavi
3	Mr. Stephen O. Onujabe	Ihima
4	Alhaji Maigida U. Lawal	Ihima
5	Alhaji Abdulrahim Momoh Jimoh	Ihima
6	Mallam Sadiq A. Ogido	Ihima
7	Alhaji U.K.A. Ibrahim	Eika
8	Alhaji S.O. Ibrahim	Eika
9	Air. Cmd. M.O Suleiman (rtd)	Eika
10	Major Yakubu Ibrahim (rtd)	Eika
11	Mallam Momoh Ibrahim	Eganyi
12	Prince haruna R. Yusuf	Okengwe
13	Mr. Samuel Musa Ozovehe	Okengwe
14	Alhaji Mohammed Otaru	Okengwe
15	Mr. Mallam Musa Otaru Sadiku	Okengwe
16	Mr. Emmanuel Onuja	Okengwe
17	Dr. Nda Aliyu	Okengwe
18	Prof. Muhammed H. Ahmed	Okengwe
19	Mallma M.J. Ohikere Zubair	Okengwe
20	Alhaji Sule Aliyu	Okengwe
21	Mallam Isyaku E. Audu	Okengwe
22	Alhaji Ismaila Yusuf	Okengwe
23	Alhaji Ahmadu A. Anivasa	Okengwe

24	Alhaji Umar Abatemi Usman	Okengwe
25	Alhaji (Dr.) Ado Ibrahim	Adavi
26	Alhaji Ibrahim Sani	Okengwe
27	Alhaji Yakubu A. Yusuf	Okengwe

APPENDIX D
NAMES OF THE TOP THREE CANDIDATES SCREENED AND THE VOTES SCORED

S/N	NAME OF ASPIRANT	VOTESSCORED
1	Alhaji (Dr.) Ado Ibrahim	Six
2	Alhaji Ibrahim Sani	Two
3	Alhaji Yakubu A. Yusuf	One

Note: Only nine of the eleven members of the council attended the screening exercise while the remaining two boycotted the meeting.

Source: GHLK/KGS/28/AD of June, 1997.

VDM publishing house ltd.

Scientific Publishing House

offers

free of charge publication

of current academic research papers, Bachelor's Theses, Master's Theses, Dissertations or Scientific Monographs

If you have written a thesis which satisfies high content as well as formal demands, and you are interested in a remunerated publication of your work, please send an e-mail with some initial information about yourself and your work to *info@vdm-publishing-house.com.*

Our editorial office will get in touch with you shortly.

VDM Publishing House Ltd.
Meldrum Court 17.
Beau Bassin
Mauritius
www.vdm-publishing-house.com

VDM Verlag Dr. Müller | LAP LAMBERT Academic Publishing | SVH Südwestdeutscher Verlag für Hochschulschriften